The Nuts and Bolts of Church Revitalization

Tom Cheyney and Terry Rials

First published by Renovate Publishing Group in 10/4/2015.

ISBN-13: **978-0990781646**

ISBN-10: **099078164X**

Printed in the United States of America

Dedication (Tom)

To Cheryl my beloved! My best friend, life companion, and one who challenges me every day to be the best I can for my Lord. You mean the world to me. There are so many things I truly admire about you as a person, as my best friend and as my wife. Your smile lights up my soul. As a church revitalizer's wife, you have been courageous to go even when the path seemed unclear and yet the hand of God was certain. You have given much and sacrificed more so others might see Jesus.

To all of those Church Revitalizers serving in local churches asking God to do great things once more and revive their church once more. The course is not easy, but the need is great and our Master longs to see the church restored for future generations.

"For God has not given us a spirit of fearfulness, but one of power, love, and sound judgment" 2 Timothy 1:7
Holman Christian Standard Bible

To God be the glory forever and ever.

Dedication (Terry)

To my wife Kay. You have been the greatest example of love, support, patience, consistency, and godly service. Thank you for going on this crazy ride in ministry. Though you are wired to stay in the background and have always desired the supportive role, you are so much more than that to me.

To Crestview Baptist Church. You have been one of the greatest blessings of my life. Our struggle to be what God wants us to be has led us to pursue revitalization. Thank you for going on this journey with me and thank you for the privilege of serving as your pastor for nearly a quarter century. Thank you for your support and your incredible love for the Lord Jesus and for me and my family.

To the pastors who have hung in there because of your calling to ministry, even when you wanted to give up. I understand. Go on this revitalization journey with us.

What Others Are Saying About *The Nuts and Bolts of Church Revitalization*

In the field of church revitalization and change, there are few experts. I should know, as I earned my PhD from Fuller Seminary in it. And one of those few experts that I highly regard is Tom Cheyney. He has not only studied the theory of church revitalization, but he has practiced it, mentoring hundreds of congregations back to health and growth. In his book, he brings together practical and effective strategies that can revitalize any church. I recommend it highly.
Bob Whitesel, DMin., PhD, Professor of Missional Leadership and founding professor of Wesley Seminary at Indiana Wesleyan University.

The need for revitalization seldom announces itself with flash and fanfare. Therefore, when the need is finally realized, where should leaders turn? Drs. Tom Cheyney and Terry Rials latest work, *The Nuts & Bolts of Church Revitalization* is the ideal first stop. Each chapter provides information and insights that will promote awareness and provide answers every church leader needs.
Rodney Harrison, Dean of Post-Graduate Studies, Professor of Christian Education, Midwestern Baptist Theological Seminary

Tom Cheyney knows churches. As a church leader himself and as an advisor to countless pastors, Tom has developed insights about church life and health that are valuable resources for all of us. In particular, Tom has a heart for church revitalization, which is one of the most pressing issues of our day. I am thankful for the investment Tom has made in helping pastors and other leaders breathe new life into dying and declining congregations.

Michael Duduit is Executive Editor of Preaching **Magazine** *and founding Dean of the Clamp Divinity School at Anderson University in Anderson, South Carolina.*

When it comes to church revitalization there is not a "One Size Fits All" approach that will work. Church revitalization is a process. In this book, Dr. Cheyney does an outstanding job presenting the nuts and bolts of church revitalization that each church can apply to its unique situation. I highly recommend this book to anyone who has a desire to see the church experience a renewed vision and passion.

Larry Wynn, Vice President, Church Revitalization, Georgia Baptist Convention

Having heard both Tom Cheney and Terry Rials speak at the Renovate National Church Revitalization Conference, it is clear that they have a lot of expertise in the area of church revitalization. It is also clear that they have a heart for the church that compels them to share what they know. If you are facing the imposing task of revitalizing your church, *The Nuts and Bolts of Church Revitalization* is a great resource.

Lee Kricher, author, For a New Generation: A Practical Guide For Revitalizing Your Church

In *The Nuts and Bolts of Church Revitalization* authors Cheyney and Rials provide essential guidance for the revitalization pastor. Both Tom Cheyney and Terry Rials are recognized national leaders in revitalization and both teach academically. What better duo to provide a pastor with biblical guidance and practical steps than men who have not only researched trends in revitalization, but also lead churches through revitalization? This is more than a philosophical approach to revitalization as some authors have given, these men are engaged in revitalization work on a personal level. This is a must read.

Kenneth Priest, Director Convention Strategies Southern Baptists of Texas Convention

Revitalization requires change and everyone knows that. But, how does the church revitalizer bring about effective change? Tom Cheyney and Terry Rials answer questions that everyone is asking, but few are answering. Cheyney is quickly becoming known as the Father of the Church Revitalization Movement and his latest book *The Nuts and Bolts of Church Revitalization* written with Terry Rials, is another great practical tool that demonstrates his unique perspective on church revitalization. Inspiring and hopeful, this is a must read for anyone who is concerned about the state of churches in North America.

Mark Weible, Director of Church Planting Greater Orlando Baptist Association

As a frequent speaker for the Renovate National Church Revitalization Conference I know these men. When it comes to church revitalization, Tom should be considered the guru of gurus. Terry Rials is one of his disciples and together they have developed this wonderful book on the nuts and bolts of church revitalization. The perspective they bring is incredibly helpful and challenging for anyone who is or wants to be involved in a church revitalization project. They do not just offer general concepts that are great in theory. Their passion for existing churches causes

them to go beyond the general ideas and present solid, practical revitalization steps anyone can take.
Jason Cooper, Pastor & Church Revitalizer of Church @ Oak Level

My friends Tom Cheyney and Terry Rials have spent the last 35 years serving the church planting and church revitalization movement. Although he speaks nationally about church revitalization and renewal, Tom is still in the middle of coaching and leading pastors in his own association in Orlando. For me personally, I learn volumes from those that are in the trenches here and now. This recent book on the nuts and bolts of church revitalization is exactly what leaders need to customize and apply these principles to their own people and community. In church life, many pastors are at a crossroads that can determine success or failure. In this new book, Tom and Terry provide some great resources for a pastor's journey to lead, renew, and grow!
Neil Franks - Lead Pastor FBC Branson - Developer of the 2-Minute Pastor Daily Video Devotional App

Like a triple latte in the early morning...we all need to be jolted from time to time. Tom Cheyney and Terry Rials specialize in this...*being jolted for the King and His Kingdom.* Do you desire to see church renewal and health in your congregation? Are you hearing others say, "it works for other churches, but not here"? Friends, church and individual revitalization is a character issue. Does the Word of God matter in your life? Do you want to see release and relief from the storms and turbulent times of your local ministry? Do you feel stuck? Tom and Terry will help you become unstuck! Is this your desire? Then you need the solid information and wisdom in this fine book. '*Desire without knowledge is not good, and whoever makes haste with his feet misses his way.*' *Proverbs 19:2* Enjoy several triple lattes, and take action on those jolts.

Greg Kappas, President, Grace Global Network & Vice President, The Timothy Initiative Author Five Stages for Multiplying Healthy Churches

Dr.'s Cheyney and Rials are national leaders and gifted speakers for the Church Revitalization Movement. They capture in *Nuts and Bolts* more than simple mechanics of church health and restoration; their instructions and insights provide the foundational pillars for the Church as it returns to its Kingdom mission in this ever-changing world.

Dr. Jim Grant, Church Revitalizer
Sr. Pastor Heartland Baptist Church

Have you ever wondered what Church Revitalization is all about? Have you ever asked questions like: What is church revitalization? How does one help revitalize a church? What does the Bible have to say about revitalization? What type of leaders are best equipped to revitalize a church? All of these questions are relevant and you are certainly not the only one asking them. The good news is this: Tom Cheyney and Terry Rials have answered these questions and so many more in their book, *The Nuts and Bolts of Church Revitalization.* You will be encouraged as they walk you through answering a variety of questions you might have concerning church revitalization. Yet, you are not just reading the theories of aspiring leaders. In this book, you hear from two of the nation's leading practitioners in

Church Revitalization. Be encouraged as you read this book, you will learn principles that will help you to become the Revitalizer that God wants you to be!
Dr. Michael Atherton Senior Pastor Cornerstone Church & author of **The Revitalized Church**

Don't bother searching the internet to borrow an idea from a church. Tom Cheyney and Terry Rials provide proven and practical tools that will help your church. I have three years' experience teaching, leading and podcasting with these guys. Their resources are extremely practical and intensely researched. No matter where you serve this is a valuable resource to help your church.
Ron Smith, Author of Churches Gone Wild

When facing the daunting task of turning your church around, starting from scratch is difficult. Tom Cheyney and Terry Rials have brought together some of the best tactics for the successful "Revitalization" of your church. This is the resource to have if you are serious about effectively "turning your situation around." Tom and Terry are real Pastor's Pastors and have a heart for your crucial role in finding a new beginning for your church. Whether you are a Senior Pastor or a church leadership team, this is a must read!
Rob Myers, Pastor of Miami Baptist Church of Miami Florida and radio personality with The Xristos Factor, President and founder of Baptist World Charities: A Global Missions Community

With the growing number of churches either plateaued or in decline in the United States, every pastor and seminary student will find their ministry in some way needing to be directed by honest and effective church renewal principles. Among the voices speaking to this issue, I am most impressed with Drs. Cheyney and Rials. Having worked for many years with Dr. Tom Cheyney and more recently with Dr. Terry Rials, I have eagerly awaited their collaboration on this new book on church renewal. Their combined expertise will inform and shape the direction of the church renewal movement for years to come. Anyone seeking to renew his or her church will be well-served by the guiding principles and insightful direction contained in these pages. I highly recommend this book to both the beginning student in church renewal as well as to the seasoned practitioner. The insights contained in this book may very well be what God uses to help you succeed in your efforts to restore the vitality and effectiveness of your own ministry as well as that of your church.

David Sundeen, Director of Online Education and Assistant Professor of Evangelism and Ministry, Midwestern Baptist Theological Seminary

Drawing from essential biblical truths, Cheyney and Rials provide insightful, rubber-meets-the-road, how-to principles for those pastors and church leaders called to lead the journey of renewal and revitalization in their particular ministry context. *"Nuts and Bolts"* offers much needed hope and encouragement – a highly recommended "must-read" resource written by two cutting edge leaders in the arena of church renewal and revitalization.

Dr. Darwin Meighan, State Director of Church Revitalization & Evangelism Nevada Baptist Convention

Table of Contents

Acknowledgements

It has been a pleasure to watch students grow to such a level that they move from being doctoral students to fellow soldiers in the cause of revitalizing churches all across North America. My friend Terry Rials has been an accomplished student and has now become a tremendous church revitalizer and practioner for this cause.

Recently, an individual who knew of the work we have done with the *RENOVATE National Church Revitalization Conference* and the supportive resources such as *The Church Revitalizer Magazine*, suggested that I write a simple yet significant book on the nuts and bolts of church revitalization and renewal. I immediately thought of Terry and asked him if he would commit to such a project. That began our journey towards creating this tool for churches of all sizes in need of church revitalization and renewal.

Each year while working with both churches locally where I live in central Florida and where Terry lives in Oklahoma City, we have been blessed to have a national multi-denominational platform through the *RENOVATE National Church Revitalization Conference* to continue to raise up the topic of church revitalization and renewal.

While there are many out there in various institutions who are brushing off their concepts from the 1970's, let's be quick to say that there is no magic pill for church revitalization and renewal, and that what works in one setting may not work in another. God desires to create a unique you. Begin the journey!

Introduction
The Seven Pillars of
Church Revitalization and Renewal

Our Lord loves the local New Testament church and it is His desire to see it grow! The need for church revitalization has never been greater in North America. An estimated 340,000 Protestant churches in America have an average attendance of less than one hundred.[1] Research data tells us that in the United States more than 80% of the churches have plateaued or are declining.[2] Each and every week we are currently seeing somewhere between fifty and seventy-five local churches closing their doors and not opening them again. Everything that must be done in the area of church revitalization cannot be accomplished in a few hours on the Lord's Day!

The most recent research data released in January of 2012 by the *Leavell Center for Evangelism and Church Health*, has said that within my own Southern Baptist Convention, we are at a critical juncture regarding church plateau and decline. The most recent series of studies have been conducted by Bill Day, Associate Director of the *Leavell Center for Evangelism and Church Health*, who serves the New Orleans Baptist Theological Seminary as the Gurney Professor of

---

[1] Hartford Institute for Religious Research (hirr.hartsem.edu/research)

[2] Research Source: Stats listed online at: http://www.newchurchinitiatives.org/morechurches/index.htm (accessed 2/23/2006).

Evangelism and Church Health. Day conducted sequential studies on church health and growth in 2003, 2007, and 2010. In January of 2012 Bill Day reported that currently there are less than seven percent (6.8) of our SBC churches that are healthy growing churches. That means a little more than 4,600 of our 45,727 SBC churches are healthy.[3] Even the number of SBC churches is in decline and we need to address the needs for church revitalization immediately.

Thinking About the Seven Pillars of Church Revitalization

Work in this regard will lead you eventually to consider the seven pillars of effective revitalization. A church revitalizer will not be working in all of these areas at the same time, but you will eventually find yourself working in most of them at one time or another. Take a moment to reflect upon the seven pillars graph as we discuss these areas of renewal and revitalization.

---

[3] http./www.bpnews.net. *Study Updates Stats On Health of Southern Baptist Churches* (accessed June, 2015).

Revitalization and Realignment

Perhaps the easiest pillar to address is revitalization and realignment. Some observers of church revitalization and renewal argue that the era of small churches is over and that the future belongs to the arising mega churches across North America. Granted, the mega-church is an amazing phenomenon of the past thirty years, which seems to have arisen with the concept of the massive campus church. But to ignore the 340,000 plus churches in North America that average less than 100 weekly in church attendance would be ill-advised! Those who serve and those who attend these churches are an enormously significant network of Christian influence. Even the mega church finds itself struggling to avoid plateau and decline.

A church in need of revitalization is described as one where: there is the plateauing or declining after a phase of recent or initial expansion followed by the beginning of a high turn-over of lay leaders. There then becomes a shorter duration of stay of fully assimilated people within the work, and the church morale and momentum level drops. The church may coast for a brief time and then momentum drops again, only to see the cycle of decline repeated again and again. The result is that the church hits a new low! This new normal is the first sign of a church in need.

Refocusing

Refocusing is the second pillar, and it helps churches that are growing but still need to set new challenges and look for new opportunities to expand their gospel witness into their target area. Questions such as, "What is your biblical purpose?" and "Why do we exist as a congregation?" must be addressed. Looking at how God showed up in the past is a good way to get the church unstuck by addressing where it has been, how God has worked and what He holds for its future. Addressing the church's focus, vision, and leading them to discover God's new direction is just the beginning of helping a congregation to begin refocusing towards the Lord's new calling plan for the church! Many a pastor today has never been taught how to grow a church and they feel quite stuck and in need of someone to come along side of them and challenge them to refocus themselves and the church!

Re-visioning

Re-visioning can be little bit harder certainly, but not as hard as the descending order of decline that will eventually lead to the *Restarting* pillar of revitalization. Have you ever seen a church that once was alive and vital begin to lose its focus and drive for the cause of Christ? That is a church that needs to work on its re-visioning strategy! Any *re-visioning* strategy works to help churches dream new dreams and accomplish new goals that lead towards re-growing a healthy church. This strategy is perfectly designed for a weekend retreat in order to foster a sense of ownership and teamwork related to discovering a shared vision for the church. Understanding the critical milestones necessary for a new vision will help foster healthy church practices that might have been lost. Something as simple as achieving a great goal of some sort can begin to launch a church back into a *re-visioning* strategy. Something as simple and yet as dangerous as the Lord's children taking an ill-advised rest can result in a slowing or stalling of the momentum into a maintenance mentality, and this can cause a church to become stuck.

Renewing

Church renewal is the forth pillar of the seven pillars of the church revitalization process. Often the church simply needs to get back to what was working and get back on track. When that is needed, a careful renewal strategy needs to be planned and carried out. Renewing a congregation becomes much harder than the refocusing, re-visioning and revitalization process. Not everyone who works in church renewal is wired the exact same way and it is important to understand each congregation's individual needs, rather than trying to make one size fit all! There is no magic pill in church revitalization. Far too much writing on church growth of the 1980's was designed in a one size fits all "bigger is better" model, and while it may not have been the only cause for declining numbers in our churches, it certainly contributed! It is vital that you prepare the laity for the work of church renewal as well as yourself. Communicate early and often with the church how the renewal process will take place and how it will be implemented. Prepare yourself spiritually and then prepare your leaders spiritually. Then begin preparing your church spiritually for renewal! A *Church Renewal Weekend* is a great way to start! Church renewal is not about finding the magic medication or treatment to get growing. It is more about discovering God's vision for the church and practicing it for the long haul. The utilization of a Church Renewal weekend works well to draw God's people back towards health and vitality.

Reinvention

This fifth pillar of Church Revitalization deals with tools and techniques that are necessary in order to assist the church in reinventing itself to a changing community. When a church experiences a shift in the community makeup, often there will be to various degrees, the need to redevelop a new experience for those who make up the new church context! New experiences must replace old experiences. New practices likewise will replace old practices. A church that is experiencing the need for reinvention must take seriously the need and make the commitment for reinventing itself, revaluing itself, reforming itself, and reinvigorating itself to fit the new context.

Restoration

This sixth area of Church Revitalization addresses the things a church and minister must go through when circumstances necessitate a restoration process! Things such as:

Gaining a new and fresh understanding of the future for the church is vital if success is in the church's future.

Inspiring new prospects with a vision that is both compelling and motivational. Prospects seek to be inspired and not dragged down in the world in which we live.

Meeting new needs in order to give you a restored place among the community in which you seek to further minister.

Becoming prospect driven during these days of transition. Look for new and yet to be reached opportunities to minister.

Remembering that if you try to do everything you will end up doing nothing. Therefore, pick your greatest opportunities first and let the rest follow along later.

Crafting something that comes out of a community in flux and looking for ways to reconnect with the community where you once were firmly entrenched. Keep in mind you have been given a second chance so don't blow it. Prayerfully seek the new things because it might be something you will be doing for a long long time!

Restarting

The final Pillar of Church Revitalization is the hardest and often only happens once the church's patriarchs and matriarchs have tried everything else they could think of to grow the church with no success. The challenge here is that most churches wait too long to enter into this area of revitalization and by the time they are willing to utilize this strategy, they have sucked out all of the life in the church and it is no longer a viable candidate for this effort. When a sick church no longer has the courage to work through the various issues that led to its poor health, it is usually identified as being on life support and in need of a restart. This type of church has been flat-lined and just holding on by means of its legacy and the faithful few who attend.

The Restarting Strategy (also known as a Repotting strategy) is intended for an unhealthy church to once again begin growing and to engage in a renewed vision that is demonstrated through sufficient evidences of hope. The restart-based church revitalization model is being used all across North America. Any group planting churches or working in the area of church revitalization should have a restart strategy if it is going to be a wise steward. One critical point from the start is a complete change of leadership and direction; this is a must for this revitalization model to be successful. Lyle Schaller reminds us that 85,000 evangelical churches are running attendance numbers fewer than 50 on

Sunday.[4] Being aware of their "critical" condition, however, is not enough. They have to become convinced they need "major" surgical treatment. One church I have worked with still believes that they have more to offer, though their decline has been meteoritic. And yet they still refuse to allow a restart to take place.

Changing the mindset of the residual membership can often be very difficult. Senior adults occupy most of these restart candidate churches for which change is often hard to come by. Until the church is ready to make drastic changes, it is useless to become involved. There are thousands of churches like this all over America: Some are Baptists, others are Methodists, even in the Assemblies you can find them, Presbyterians, the Lutherans have them, Congregational, Christian, and many others, waiting for a mission-minded congregation to get involved in offering "new life."

A startling phenomenon is occurring in some churches today wherein laity who begin to depart this life see nothing wrong with taking the church to the grave as well. That was never part of God's plan for the very thing for which He gave up His life.

---

[4] C.f. Schaller, Lyle E. *A Mainline Turnaround. Strategies for Congregations and Denominations.* Nashville: Abingdon. 2005.

CHAPTER 1
FAST FACTS FOR THE BUSY PASTOR

While leading RenovateConference.org, I have realized the hard reality in North America that most churches and most, if not all, denominations are in a state of decline. The membership within these churches and denominations is plateauing and what used to pass for involvement and activity within churches is deteriorating. While all of this is happening, the rank and file of the church appear powerless to assemble the strength that is needed to get the churches growing again. Kevin Ezell, President of the North American Mission Board of the Southern Baptist Convention declares, "We must keep our denominations focused on the ministry of rebirth and redemption, not on the business of enforcing rules and rituals."[5] In 1990 an editor for the *Wall Street Journal* Wade Clark Roof published an editorial article entitled, "The Episcopalian Goes the Way of the Dodo," where he argued the decline of mainline denominationalism and its effect on Christianity.[6] With the turn of the twenty-first century, sustained growth within our churches is an intermittent exception while decline seems to be more of the pronouncement. The mainline denominations

---

[5] David S. Dockery, Ray Van Neste, and Jerry Tidwell, *Southern Baptists, Evangelicals and the Future of Denominationalism* (Nashville: B&H Publishing Group, 2011), i.

[6] Wade Clark Roof, "The Episcopalian Goes the Way of the Dodo," *Wall Street Journal*, July 20, 1990.

to which Roof referred, are still in the midst of severe decline and serious deterioration. Stuck in the status quo, new wine cannot be poured into the same old wine skins of outdated mindsets. A new sense of urgency is required for lasting change. Change is required and a church in need of revitalization and renewal cannot escape change. Will we allow the church of America to become mirrors of the churches all across Europe that find themselves empty urns holding the obvious? We must not.

The need for training and equipping today's minister with the tools and skill sets necessary to combat this rampant plateau and decline is crucial. Most ministers coming out of our seminaries today lack preparation for the challenge of church revitalization and renewal. If the estimates are accurate, that at least eighty percent or more of our churches are in need of revitalization, then it stands to reason that the majority of graduates from our seminaries are going to begin their ministries in the majority of these churches. Less than five percent of these graduates will actually be going to healthy churches. Existing ministers will pastor the healthy pool of churches that make up the twenty percent so the seminarian needs to prepare for the eventual challenge of revitalizing a plateaued or declining church.

THE TIME IS RIGHT NOW!

If there is going to be revitalization in American churches in the twenty-first century, the initial step must be taken immediately. Revitalization of our southern Baptist churches is not an insurmountable task. While we must start with re-encountering the divine and recognizing that any church that is revitalized or becoming revitalized is the work of our Lord God, we must also do our part to provide tools and methodologies for today's ministers to assist them with new practices and approaches that can help today's declining church. Our southern Baptist churches must not remain in stained glass, red-bricked, spire castles giving out apologies for lack of renewal or mixed gestures towards revitalization efforts.

The time for revitalization and renewal is now for sick and declining churches are all across America. Will the people of God be lead like days of old when the shepherds of God boldly served the church of God, and led His people to remember why they exist and to whom they belong? With such an absence of missionary mandates from our missionary agencies, the challenge is for the theological institutions across the convention to pick up the slack and prepare the new army of church revitalizers.

STATISTICS ARE OUR FRIENDS IN CHURCH REVITALIZATION AND RENEWAL

According to *Leadership Journal*, 340,000 churches are in need of church revitalization today.[7] Ninety-five

---

[7] http://www.ctlibrary.com/le/2005/fall/8.24.html (accessed 3/20/11).

percent of churches in North America average 100 or less. Over eighty percent of American churches are in decline or on a plateau. Each year, approximately 3,500 churches die in North America.[8] Within my own Southern Baptist Convention the annual death rate averages between seven and nine hundred![9] Studies have shown that churches typically plateau in attendance by their fifteenth year, and by year 35 they begin having trouble replacing the members they lose."[10] Only 7.3% of small churches are growing in North America currently. Of the churches that are fifty years old or older, only 9.2% are growing.

In North America, fifty to sixty churches close their doors every week. Among churches of all sizes, growing churches are rare! In fact, some research indicates that they only make up about "20 percent of our churches today. The other 80 percent have reached a plateau or are declining."[11] In a study of more than two thousand churches, David Olson revealed that 69 percent of our churches in America

---

[8] Warren Bird, "More Churches Opened Than Closed in 2006," *Rev Magazine,* July-August 2007, 68.

[9] *"Annual Change in the Number of Southern Baptist Churches 1973-2009"* Center for Missional Research, North American Mission Board, SBC. Alpharetta, Georgia.

[10] "Churches Die with Dignity" *Christianity Today* Jan. 1991, Vol. 36.

[11] Stetzer, Ed and Warren Bird, *Viral Churches: Helping Church Planters Become Movement Makers* (San Francisco: Jossey-Bass, 2010), 60.

have reached a plateau or even worse are declining.[12] Jim Tomberlin and Warren Bird declare that "80 percent of the three hundred thousand Protestant churches in the United States have plateaued or are declining, and many of them are in desperate need of a vibrant ministry."[13] The majority of these churches have fewer than two hundred people in attendance and a large portion have fewer than seventy-five weekly.[14]

This Southern Baptist research arm within the denomination; LifeWay Christian Resources, in cooperation with the Center for Missional Research from the North American Mission Board, conducted a study based on churches' five-year change in total membership. The study reports that 28.1 percent of our Southern Baptist Convention churches are growing, 43.9 percent are in a state of plateau, and 28 percent are in decline.[15]

---

[12] David T. Olson, *The American Church in Crisis* (Grand Rapids: Zondervan Publishing, 2008), 132.

[13] Tomberlin, Jim and Warren Bird, *Better Together: Making Church Mergers Work* (San Francisco: Jossey-Bass, 2010), xvi.

[14] "Fast Facts." Hartford Institute for Religion Research. Retrieved from http://hirr.hartsem.edu/research/fastfacts/fast_facts.html#size cong (accessed 3/20/2011).

[15] Annual Church Profile data, LifeWay Christian Resources, Nashville, TN.Compiled by: Center for Missional Research, North American Mission Board, Alpharetta, GA.

A more recent series of studies were conducted by Bill Day, Associate Director of the Leavell Center for Evangelism and Church Health, who serves the New Orleans Baptist Theological Seminary as the Gurney Professor of Evangelism and Church Health. In his sequential studies on church health and growth from 2003, 2007, and 2010, he reports that currently there are less than seven percent (6.8) of our SBC churches which are healthy growing churches. That means 3,087 of our 45,727 SBC churches are healthy.[16] Leonard Sweet states that the declining mainline church has faced a "double whammy of post-modernity and post-Christendom."[17]

---

[16] Bill Day. *The State of the Church in the S.B.C.* (New Orleans: Leavell Center for Evangelism and Church Health, 1/3/2012), C.f. Appendix Two.

[17] Leonard Sweet. *So Beautiful: Divine Design for Life and the Church* (Colorado Springs: David C. Cook, 2009), 20.

CHAPTER 2
The Task of Church Revitalization

In my own revitalization work, I have personally noticed that the church in America is in big trouble – which is exactly what all the statisticians are saying. The church has been in a serious decline for a long time. Scholars cannot even agree when the decline began, but southern Baptist churches have experienced a steady decline in baptismal rates since 1956, its banner year. It has been sliding downhill since. In the last decade, southern Baptist churches have seen church membership decline by 10%, Sunday School attendance decrease by 15%, baptisms drop over 30%, and the number of people joining Baptist churches plummet by nearly 50%! It's easy to talk about the churches somewhere else that are experiencing this, but this phenomenon is hitting too close to home. We have this problem right here in our communities. As I look at the statistics, it's happening to nearly ninety percent of the churches in the Association, maybe even to the one to which you belong.

The Steady Decline

What are we doing about this steady decline? Some sit around and talk about the 'good old days' and do nothing because they don't agree with what is happening. Some ascribe blame to others, and we've seen plenty of that. Some blame those who hold to an old, outmoded traditionalism, which isn't working anymore. Some blame the mega churches of stealing members from smaller churches. Some blame their pastor or denominational leaders for the decline. Some blame the lack of door-to-door evangelism, the lack of church revivals, the lack of discipleship training programs, or failure of the church to keep up with culture. The truth is – there is enough blame to go around. For many of you, this is the first time you've heard of this problem.

As in the days of Nehemiah, we need to look around at our crumbling walls and discover that we are a reproach to the name of our Lord.[18] A reproach is a condition of shame, an occasion given to the enemy for him to exult in our defeat. Every Sunday with an empty parking lot, an empty building, and empty altar is a reproach to his name. We need earnest repentance, honest admission, and public confession.[19] The problem is with us, all of us.

The good news is that leaders are addressing this problem like never before. We learned that it doesn't come from a national movement; we've seen plenty of those in the past fifty years. The Church Growth Movement, the Church Health Movement, the Missional Church Movement, and the Emerging Church Movement have each tried to turn the church around, so far with very limited success. The real pattern for success is the biblical one, alluded to by famed preacher G. Campbell Morgan, who metaphorically challenged young preachers to put their sailboats out into the water, put up the sail and

---

[18] Nehemiah 1:3.

[19] Nehemiah 2:17.

wait for the wind to blow. We need a movement of God, but the wind of God isn't blowing, or is it?

Setting the Sails

I would like to explore the journey of leading churches back to vitality and life. We'll explore how to set the sails and wait for the wind of God to blow.

The church is like a sailboat, as sailboats in and of themselves are powerless. It has been said that without the wind, a sailboat can only claim the title of organized driftwood. It has no engine, no motor, and no oarsmen. The sailboat is completely dependent upon the wind, in fact, it is *designed* to harness the wind. The church is powerless without the presence and work of the Holy Spirit. The church was designed to catch the wind of revival. The upper room disciples felt the mighty rushing wind and in a matter of hours they changed the world.[20]

Like a sailboat with no wind, the church without the Holy Spirit will simply float, because it has no power behind it. Most churches can function in their normal program and ministry for an indefinite period of time without the work of the Holy Spirit because most churches are not leaning on Him. To be sure, a few churches have had their lamp removed, which

---

[20] Dan Jarvis, "Set The Sails," *Life Action Ministries* (blog), September 1, 2004, http://www.lifeaction.org/revival-resources/revive/setting-sails/set-sails/ (last accessed July 27, 2015).

Jesus threatened to do in Revelation 2:5. These churches will surely die. Sadly, when God's presence leaves, it is possible to be completely unaware of it. For example, Samson did not realize that the Lord had left him after his hair was cut.[21] Could the church be unaware that His glory has departed?

Should we just shut down some of these weak or sick churches that are going to die anyway? Some argue that revitalization is a futile effort because as Bill Easum puts it, "The only solution for spiritually dead congregations is resurrection. You cannot revitalize something that is dead. They must be brought to life again!"[22] You already know that Southern Baptists have no authority over any local church. Some Baptist leaders suggest that these churches should close their doors or give their property away to another church or mission, which is honorable, or find some other way to continue in ministry. In numerous conversations with pastors, I sense that pastors and churches are seeking permission to die; however we're on a slippery slope because once we start scuttling churches in trouble, your church may be next.

God can revive, refresh, and renew the church any time He chooses to do so. We are praying that He does just that and soon. Revival is the extraordinary work of the Holy Spirit producing extraordinary

---

[21] Judges 16:20.

[22] Bill Easum, *A Second Resurrection: Leading Your Congregation to New Life* (Nashville: Abingdon Press, 2007), 8.

results…the re-entry of Christ's manifest presence, according to Richard Owen Roberts. It overthrows the status quo and refreshes His kingdom purposes on earth. Revitalization is the work we do to ensure that the conditions of God are met for revival and in order that the people of God are prepared when the Sovereign God begins to move.

Beginning the Task of Revitalization

How do we begin the task of church revitalization? Let's start by creating an environment or habitat for revitalization to happen. It takes some cultivation to produce a healthy garden, and it takes some careful cultivation and a healthy environment within the church to turn the church around. Even if the church is sick, weak, plateaued, or declining, it can have a healthy attitude going into a revitalization project.

First, churches must create an environment that is safe for their pastor to lead this effort. From my research, I have discovered most pastors do not know what to do, or if they do, they are afraid to do it. If they don't know what to do, they aren't confident to lead their churches in revitalization. The pastor of today's church needs specialized training and ministry coaches if he hopes to turn the church around. Additionally, sometimes pastors are afraid to address problems in the church out of fear – fear of confronting sin in the church, fear of losing people, fear of committing to the three-year process of revitalization, or fear of losing their jobs. Churches can be a hostile environment – 1,600 evangelical pastors leave the ministry each month in the United States. Put another way, 90% of all pastors will not stay in ministry until retirement.[23] Did you know that pastors are not eligible for unemployment insurance?

Second, in order for a church to experience revitalization, it must develop an environment of spiritual honesty and confession. Nehemiah was honest when he told the Jerusalemites, "You see the bad situation we are in…"[24] The *Halo Effect* is the tendency to speak about the church or spiritual issues in only a favorable light. If you ask most preachers or church members about their church attendance, they will often give a number that is better than reality. It is possible that they truly believe what they say and do not intend to be deceptive. The reality, however, is that most people in the church simply do not know the numbers. The Sunday School placards are long gone from most sanctuaries because we don't want to look at the bad news. One-third of our churches do not even report their data to the convention at all.[25] Is your church completing and submitting its annual

---

[23] Richard J. Krejcir, "Statistics On Pastors: What Is Going On with the Pastors in America?", Into Thy Word, 2007, accessed July 27, 2015, http://www.intothyword.org/apps/articles/default.asp?articleid=36562.

[24] Nehemiah 2:17.

[25] The writer makes this general observation from research of associational church reporting to the Southern Baptist Directory Service over the last ten years.

church profile? We have to get honest with ourselves.

Third, and most importantly, we have to create an environment of prayer. Prayer meetings are too often "organ recitals;" we pray for people's body parts. Intercessory prayer is important, but it should include the life and health of the church. We need prayers of confession that plead with God to change us. Prayer is developing an intimacy with the God who saves us. Pray for personal renewal first before you pray for revitalization of the church. Some of the greatest revivals in history came when people prayed and earnestly confessed their sins before God.

The Need to Train Church Revitalizers

Not every leader can help a declining organization turnaround and thrive again. The business world has known this for quite some time. Businesses can go out, find these amazing leaders, and hire them away from other corporations. They can offer exorbitant salaries because leaders with these skills are well worth their investment! Of course, the church cannot just hire its leaders like CEOs; leaders of the church are shepherds, called into ministry by God, gifted by the Holy Spirit, empowered with the authority of the Word of God, and called by a church to serve. A large percentage of the pastoral leadership in the church today has never had any training in revitalization leadership.

Our Renovate Church Revitalization leadership team is convinced that leaders of today's church can be equipped in this task of church revitalization. This training was never a part of their college and seminary training. When these church leaders were trained, the church field was very different than the field is today. We were in the midst of a great time of church expansion, called the Church Growth Movement. Sadly, that time of expansion is over.

Some churches cannot wait around for academia to train the next generation of pastoral leaders; they need help right now! Many of our pastors know their churches are in trouble and need this training today. Churches often know they are in trouble, but do not know where to begin. Some churches blame their pastors and falsely assume that a new pastor is the solution, but it is doubtful that a new pastor will instantly solve the problems that a church has had for years. Our predicament is just that – our predicament. Let's stop assigning blame and begin looking for solutions. Pastors make plenty of mistakes, and as a pastor I freely admit that, but church members make mistakes too. Think of it this way – your current pastor is or can be the best pastor you'll ever have. Let's get behind our pastors and go to work alongside them to turn these churches around!

Our Renovate Church Revitalization Group is developing training for pastors and key church leaders as we speak. I have a significant role in developing this training. The training consists of two primary topics, revival and revitalization. Revival is the extraordinary work of the Holy Spirit producing extraordinary results. God can decide to revive His church at any time, and I hope He does, because

America has not had a sustained nationwide revival in over 100 years, the longest spiritual drought in our history. And there is a reason for it. We need to do the work to ensure that the conditions of God are met for revival so the church is prepared when the Sovereign God begins to move. That is revitalization! I pray this is the beginning of a great movement of God in our day, but we have obstacles to overcome.

Obstacles to Overcome

The church revitalization process has several obstacles to overcome. These obstacles are scary to face and difficult to address. The first set of obstacles a church must overcome includes pride, selfishness, and self-deception. Gary McIntosh, in his book *Overcoming the Dark Side of Leadership*, says that the very first human leadership failure was the result of these sins. These very sins led to the fall of man, which resulted in their separation from perfect fellowship with God.[26] The same is true today. Our sins keep us from the fellowship with God that He intends. Our plateaued and declining churches have wonderful people in them who truly love God, but perhaps we have forgotten that the church is a missionary body that seeks the redemption of the lost at all costs. We should not delude ourselves any longer. With nearly 90% of our churches plateaued and declining, we

---

[26] Gary L. McIntosh and Samuel D. Rima, *Overcoming the Dark Side of Leadership: How to Become an Effective Leader by Confronting Potential Failures* (Grand Rapids: Baker Books, 2007), 59-63.

must reject our pride, take ownership of our problems, and address our situations honestly and directly.

The second set of obstacles to revitalization includes the problems of entrenched leadership, church passivity, and congregational age, which are all related. These take a bit more explanation. Churches owe a debt of gratitude to many people who have been faithful and supportive of their churches for years, but because few new people come into the church, there are very few new leaders in the church. Existing leaders can become entrenched and take too much ownership of their positions, which drives away potential new leaders. These entrenched leaders can become a real obstacle to growth. They may resist or even oppose pastoral leadership and can be threatened if new ways are suggested. They can exert control, become watchdogs of the pastor and staff, and assume responsibility to preserve the traditions of the church. This situation is repeated over and over again. The truth is, churches truly love these members, and they should, but failing to address our entrenched leadership problem hurts the church. Long-term leadership also creates passivity, which stems from long-term leaders becoming tired. They become passive and often do the minimum that is required. These people are not entrenched leaders, they are just exhausted. New leadership brings new ideas, new ways, and new energy for the church. If churches do not grow, then the congregation just gets older – together. In general, the older congregation finds itself in more trouble than a younger one. By far, the healthiest churches in America are multigenerational churches with every age proportionally represented, and those with a steady influx of new leadership. We must admit that some change is necessary and good, and many churches will be helped with some newness. The Renovate Church Revitalization team wants to help churches address these problems; we have amazing leadership and proven ways to help churches to do this.

It Is Time to Fix the Hole

The plateaued and declining church needs to do something. Church and denominational leaders need to do something. We have spent enough time ringing the bell, shouting that there is a hole in the boat. It's time to fix the hole. The more I study the existing church, the more convinced I am that the people in the pews want to see their churches turn around too. There is some disagreement on what must happen, but I would say that most are ready for some positive change. Here is some sage advice:

First and foremost, pray about church revitalization. Pray and seek God's face for this undertaking. Nehemiah prayed both day and night for four months before he ever took action.[27] Nehemiah's first recorded prayer began with praise, proceeded to intercession for his people, and ended in confession of sin, both his own and those of his people.[28] For a man so well known for his actions, Nehemiah spent a

---

[27] Nehemiah 1:4,6.

[28] Nehemiah 1:5-7.

great deal of time being still in prayer before the Lord.

Second, affirm your pastor and his leadership in the church. The vast majority of pastors love their churches and work very hard in their callings. He is probably doing the best he can, but he may just need to hear this – that you and other key leaders will work with him to renew the church. He cannot make these changes by himself. Most pastors do not know what to do to revitalize their churches, so encourage your pastor to seek specialized training in revitalization, which the Renovate National Church Revitalization Conference makes available to the pastors.

Third, get to the point that you and your pastor can speak about your circumstances openly and at length with the church. Nothing is worse than attempting to effect change without the help and support of the congregation. If the congregation does not know about the problems, how can they help to fix them? Do not form another committee to study and report back to the church. A revitalization team is needed, but that comes later.

Fourth, do not be afraid to ask for outside help. One dangerous consequence of pride is the inability to ask for help from others. Your pastor will need help from coaches to guide him into and through this process. The church will need help from sister churches coming alongside to help! The Renovate Church Revitalization team is asking that some of our stronger churches to help, or even to adopt, struggling congregations.

Fifth, address the opposition that comes from revitalization biblically and swiftly. The devil hates the church moving in the right direction. Conflict will come from within and without, just ask Nehemiah! Confess sin and confront sin. Some churches are sick because there is sin in the camp. Stay ever-vigilant and learn about spiritual warfare, because it is coming.

Your Church's Life Cycle

Let's talk church revitalization. We begin by assessing where the church is in its life cycle.

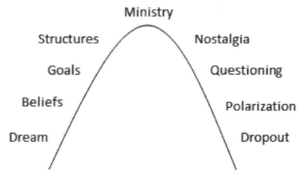

Let us take a cursory look at where *your* church is in its life cycle. Robert Dale developed a very simple model to help us to understand your church's situation. Your church is in one of these nine categories in the figure above. The ultimate goal is ministry, but in order to get there, a church must have a dream about effective ministry. Out of that dream comes a clarification of their beliefs and goals, and then structures are developed to help them to do their peak ministry. Regrettably, decline begins when the church becomes nostalgic and longs to return to its comfortable past. The church begins to assign blame for its decline and then becomes polarized over its future leadership and direction. Eventually, a long, steady stream of people begins to drop out of the church. Put simply, a church should attempt to stay on the left side of this curve. When peak ministry is achieved, the church needs to dream again in order to stay on the left side of the curve.[29]

Dream a New Dream

Dreaming a new dream for a church in need of revitalization is quite different than one for a healthy, thriving one. In church life today we call this *vision*. The biblical Nehemiah was deeply moved when he heard the sad report about the destruction of Jerusalem. For many days he mourned and prayed over the situation caused by the people's sins, including his own. Out of his awareness of the need and his immersion in prayer, Nehemiah developed the conviction that God's people, who had just returned to their land, must honor God by rebuilding the city walls of Jerusalem and stop being a reproach to the name of the Lord.

As the vision formed to rebuild the walls, Nehemiah realized that he himself had been called to carry it out. Frequently, those who form such a vision for their church will be called by God to fulfill it. This

---

[29] Robert Dale, *To Dream Again: How to Help Your Church Come Alive* (Nashville: Broadman Press), 1983.

is an important concept in revitalization leadership –
calling comes *out of* vision! Put church revitalization
into a formula, it would go something like this:

Nehemiah was a man of vision who could see
the possibilities of what could happen if he
surrendered to the will of God. Someone once said,
"Vision is the ability to see the possibilities of what
could happen if you surrender to the will of God, the
ability to see what God wants in your day."

Let me walk you through some steps to help you
develop a vision for revitalization. First, begin praying
– Nehemiah did. He spent four months praying
before he ever shared his plan with the King of
Persia.[30] Second, after much, much prayer, share your
vision and the reason for your motivation.[31] Third,
give your testimony of how God has dealt with you
about leading your church to renewal because every
vision has a backdrop.[32] Fourth, test the vision to see
if there is the proper response among those with
whom you serve.[33]

---

[30] Nehemiah 1:4-2:4.

[31] Nehemiah 2:17.

[32] Nehemiah 2:18.

[33] Nehemiah 2:18.

Do not let this one fact escape your attention – Nehemiah was an unknown commodity to the people in Jerusalem. Most revitalizers are people of obscurity whom no one would expect to lead out in this way. It is highly doubtful that anyone in Jerusalem knew Nehemiah, aside from his own family.

Though an unknown in Jerusalem, Nehemiah understood the principles of authority. When he sensed his calling to rebuild the walls, he worked *with* the authorities already in place (King Artaxerxes, the King's officials, the governors of the provinces, etc.). The people followed Nehemiah and began to rebuild the walls because they knew he had been with God, received his calling from God, worked within existing authority structures, and effectively communicated his vision. If you have this calling to revitalize your church, the people will follow you too.

How Revitalizers Begin to Assess a Church's Problems

Nehemiah's calling to rebuild the walls of Jerusalem came from hearing about (not seeing) the destruction of Jerusalem's gates and his people there living in reproach. The report he received from his brother about the sad condition of the city was the first news of the city's situation. By the time Nehemiah finally reached Jerusalem, eight months had elapsed; he spent four months in prayer before asking leave of the Persian King and it took four months to travel to Jerusalem from Susa, the Western capital of Persia. We should learn from Nehemiah –

never rush the process of revitalization! O.S. Hawkins once said, "Those who get the job of rebuilding done do not rush in before they do their homework. They take a good long look at the situation for themselves. It is a part of the price of leadership."[34]

Even after arriving in Jerusalem, Nehemiah was slow to start the work. His first task was to assess the situation first-hand. He was certainly briefed by his brothers, but that is quite different from one's own personal assessment. When he reached Jerusalem, Nehemiah waited three more days before announcing his intentions. It was then that Nehemiah made his famous nighttime ride to survey the walls.

Scripture is remarkably silent about what transpired in those three days, but Nehemiah probably spent time in prayer; he had done so for months prior. He probably wanted to assess the situation privately before presenting this grand project to the officials and the people. He probably met with the leaders, including the spiritual leaders of the Jewish community. He probably spent part of the time evaluating the spiritual condition of people and their leadership potential. He probably had to decide what parts of the wall were going to be rebuilt and which ones were not.

[34] O. S. Hawkins, "Rebuilding: Rebuilders Build a Team Spirit - Part 2", accessed July 20, 2015, http://www.oshawkins.com/sermons/rebuilders-build-a-team-spirit/.

When we look at Nehemiah's pattern for revitalization leadership we are struck with the realization that we too must assess the problems in our church. What are the problems, obstacles, and sins that keep our churches from vitality and fruitfulness? The most frequent question we are asked in church revitalization is, "What is the problem with the church today?" I wish we had a simple answer. If every person who went to the doctor had the same illness, then prescribing the right treatment would be easy because what worked for one person would be good for the next. The sickness and ugliness in our churches today are often similar, but are too varied and individual to address them the same way.

Diagnosing the problem with the church is an important step. Church Revitalizers are working hard to help our church leaders to diagnose their problems. We have some incredible tools available to us today that help with that diagnosis. We are encouraging church leaders to pursue the path of revival and awakening in their churches. We are working hard to develop well-trained revitalization leaders in our churches. We are here to help churches to develop and to implement their own scripturally-based, strategic plans to address these problems and sins.

However, just because a church is aware of their problems does not necessarily mean they are ready to address them. Someone once said that until the pain of remaining the same outweighs the pain of change, nothing will happen in the life of the church. The Renovate Church Revitalization Group has incredible tools to help churches and leaders to assess their problems and readiness for change. What can you do today to help your church and others like it to begin to experience renewal? Begin praying for that very thing right now. Encourage your pastor and church leaders to trust in the power of God to change our hearts. Resist the temptation to think that revitalization is a mechanical process that we can accomplish apart from God's refreshing Spirit. Unless the wind blows, the sailboat is powerless!

Developing Revitalization Leadership

Churches seem to have the same questions about revitalization, and they are very good questions. I would briefly like to answer some of the more common ones:

1. What is church revitalization?

Revitalization is the work church leaders do to ensure that the conditions of God are met for revival, so that the people of God are prepared when He begins to move. Other denominations often use the term "renewal." Technically, renewal describes the experience that first comes to the individual who experiences a spiritual refreshing from God. Revitalization is a term that describes the experience of the church.

2. How does the Renovate Group Church Revitalization Team help churches in the revitalization?

We help churches to assess their revitalization issues and their readiness to enter into the revitalization process. We offer training for your pastor and church leadership in revitalization and assist them in developing and implementing a revitalization strategy. We provide a revitalization consultant to walk with your pastor and church through the process. We also begin a coaching relationship with the pastor and provide a personal coach.

3. How does the Renovate Group help churches diagnose their problems and concerns?

The Renovate Church Revitalization Group has some excellent diagnostic instruments and fully-trained coaches, consultants, and staff to assist your church. We can provide your church with a community demographic profile and community surveys to help you to understand your community's ministry needs.

4. How long does it take to see revitalization in the church?

The revitalization process will take a minimum of 1,000 days, but some of the changes will come very soon in the process; others take much more time to fully implement. At the end of the 1,000 days, the church should have embraced the revitalization and the healthier ways of worshipping, serving, and ministering will become the new normal.

5. How much does church revitalization cost financially?

The good news is that very minimal expenses, if any, are involved.

6. How many ways are there to revitalize the church?

There are many strategies, but what works in one church setting will not necessarily work in another. Sometimes a church disbands and donates their properties to another work or they shut down the church and restart it a few weeks later with new leadership in place. A church may move to a new facility or relocate to another area to reach its target demographic (can be expensive). Some churches have favored merging with another church, a strategy that is rarely successful. The church may decide to share its facilities with another work, which allows it to share its expenses as well. The church may plan to transition its existing church into a new work, especially when the community experiences demographic changes. A church may decide to go back under mission status after seeking out a healthy sponsoring church.

7. Has this process worked in other churches?

Yes it has! Though we've only had Church

Revitalization Teams for a short period of time, we are seeing some definite progress. For example, one church in our church revitalization network has experienced a 50% increase in attendance in one year after many years of plateau.

The Pastor and Revitalization

Let us talk briefly about your pastor and church revitalization. Virtually all experts agree that the primary responsibility for leading the church in revitalization falls upon the pastor. In this discipline, leadership is everything.

However, in most instances, if the pastor knew what to do he would do it. The difficulty lies in the fact that the church has begun a downward spiral with one problem propagating another. A declining, or plateaued church has experienced the loss of church membership, workers, and givers. Everyone knows that the church needs workers and givers to reach people. Even if the church is not losing membership or workers, the church that is not growing and reaching new, young families is a church that is just getting older together. How does a pastor lead a congregation that is plateaued, declining, or getting older?

Today's pastor needs to be something of an expert in leading congregational change, which is required if we are to see revitalization occur in the life of the church. The required change is the kind that occurs in the hearts of the people. Simply doing what we used to do, doing it better, or working harder is not the answer. We need God to break our hearts for the people of our community. We need to ask God to change us, so we can reach the current generation. Those we are trying to reach in the millennial generation think quite differently than those in the congregation. The things that are important to us are not as important to them. Attending is just as valuable to them as belonging is to us. Millennials do not value church membership as we do. I am not suggesting that the church change its gospel or its theology, but our approach may need adjusting if we are to reach this generation.

Today's pastor needs your prayer support. Ask any pastor and he will tell you that the task of pastoring today is much more challenging than it was just twenty years ago. The demands placed upon the pastor have never been greater. Satan knows how to keep churches from being revitalized. He attacks churches by attacking the pastors. Pray like never before for your pastor, your church may depend upon it.

Today's pastor needs his church to help him do the things only pastors can do, like leading the congregation and the church staff. He will tell you that he can be the pastor, but he cannot be the church. The church must step up and shoulder many of the responsibilities left at the feet of the pastor. The problem of the church in Acts 6 was that not enough time was available for those who lead through prayer and the ministry of the Word. Your pastor has the same problem, I assure you. What would happen in your church if your pastor was refreshed? If he had 50% more time for prayer and sermon preparation, I think you'd see a different man in the pulpit.

Today's pastor needs to connect with other leaders to help him focus on revitalization in his church setting. Encourage your pastor to seek training in revitalization, a specialized discipline in leadership. Business leaders who are able to lead Fortune 500 companies back into profitability are highly sought and amply compensated because there are so few who can lead revitalization. I am convinced that revitalization leadership is a skill that can be learned.

The Universal Need

The need for church revitalization is universal; churches everywhere, both at home and abroad, struggle with vitality and effectiveness. This very morning, I received a phone call from a missionary in Panama who asked for help with one of the churches there. They were looking for someone who could help them to "reinvent" their church. The problem is that the church does not want to depart from their comfortable traditions. Einstein is credited with saying, "Doing the same thing over and over again expecting different results is the definition of insanity."

Let me give a couple of illustrations. First, think of a dog chasing its tail. We have all seen a dog do this! Sometimes the dog can do it for a very long time. You would think all that spinning would leave the poor dog dizzy, if not nauseated. On occasion, a dog may actually catch its tail, at which point the spinning stops. All that is achieved is a mouthful of tail, not much of an accomplishment and not much of a reward. Churches are very active today, but maybe their activity is not the most productive. They spin around and around and rarely accomplish anything, and when they do, all they have accomplished is an unsatisfying reward. Having church is never as exciting as being the church. Keeping the lights on and the doors open are not commandments that Jesus left to the church. Are we making disciples of all nations or just spinning around, chasing our tails? Second, think of the merry-go-round on a playground. It goes round and round. As a kid, I used to imagine that while I was spinning around that I was actually in a race where I was in the lead. Honestly, I have never been fleet of foot, so it may have been a fantasy to actually win a race. Now that I'm considerably older, I understand that I was never leading anything, neither was I in second, third, or last place. We are never really in competition if we are all in the same situation. When will churches recognize that the church down the street is not our competition? We are all on the same team! We should think of them as our fellow workers in the gospel. Each church has its unique ministry and reaches a unique audience – that is how God puts the body of Christ together.

Let us stop chasing our tails with the wrong activity. Let's get off the merry-go-round of thinking that we're in first place, or the woe-is-me thinking that we are in last place. I'm not certain that "reinventing" the church is the solution. I think the church that Jesus established was given all that it needed to accomplish its mission on Earth and bring Him glory in Heaven. We have the command in scripture, "Cease striving and know that I am God."[35] Isaiah also reminds us of our real problem in the contemporary church (emphasis mine), "In repentance and rest you will be saved, in quietness and trust is your strength. But you were not willing."[36] Pray that God will break our hard-heartedness and renew His church in our day. May the Lord bless you as you seek Him.

---

[35] C.f. Psalms 46:10.

[36] C.f. Isaiah. 30:15.

CHAPTER 3
The Biblical Foundation for Church Revitalization

While leading ChurchRevitalizer.com I have noticed that pastors rarely have training in revitalization leadership, though the majority of pastoral situations are in need of revitalization. The good news is that the scriptures provide a sufficient mandate to strengthen and restore existing churches. The scriptures also provide a pattern to follow in training church revitalization leadership. Using both testaments of scripture, we will discover God's plan for revitalization, first for Israel and Judah, and then for His church. We will examine the root causes of the decline of the church, and what Jesus, Paul, and other New Testament writers instruct the church to do about it. We will discover the importance of seeking and pursuing God's glory and the value of its passionate pursuit to the work of church revitalization.

Before we explore the biblical foundation for church revitalization, we should make sure that we understand the important terms associated with church revitalization. Notice that our work is revitalization; God's work is refreshing, renewing, reviving, awakening, and reforming.

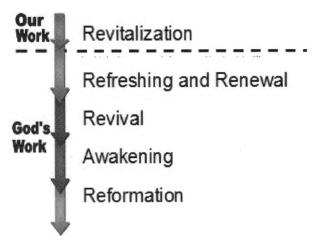

Revitalization

The work leaders do in preparing others for the work that only God can do.

Renewal & Refreshing

Renewal describes the experience that first comes to the individual who experiences a spiritual *refreshing* from God's presence. Renewal and refreshing are very similar terms with only subtle differences between them. Whereas *revival* describes a corporate experience, renewal describes the experience that first comes to the individual who experiences a spiritual refreshing from God's presence.

Revival

Revival has been defined by evangelist Vance Havner as, "...a work of God among Christians, bringing them to conviction, repentance, confession, restitution, reconciliation, separation from the world and submission to the Lordship of Christ."

Awakening

Awakening describes the need for the church to wake up, to see how far it has drifted, and to renew its passion for Jesus. *Revival* comes to the church; *awakening* comes to the nation.

Reformation

Reformation is a consequence of revival that comes to God's people and then to the lost. It changes the culture, even governments, as in the Protestant Reformation, which changed Europe and the world!

Biblical Decay

Spiritual degradation is common and universal. Churches tend to abandon biblical ideals and pursue destructive behaviors. Decay can happen very quickly. Both Testaments of scripture argue for revitalization because spiritual degradation is common and universal. Israel, and later, Judah, experienced periods of decline and apostasy. The church later experienced the same phenomenon after its establishment. Scripture addresses this problem extensively. Jesus, Jude, Peter, and Paul address issues that are important to the discussion of revitalization. So destructive in fact that not one of the churches established in the pages of the New Testament survives to the present. All the churches listed in the New Testament, including those in Judea, Syria, Galatia, Macedonia, Achaia, Mysia, Asia, and others, succumbed to stagnation, entropy, and death. This was certainly not Jesus' intent for His church. If a church is not moving forward, it is probably moving backward. Eventually, it will succumb to entropy, the tendency of anything to wind down and move toward disorder. Other researchers have noticed this same phenomenon, such as Arnold Cook, who describes this as *historical drift*.[37] Decay can happen very quickly.

Organizational decay, or even abandonment of faith, does not take a great deal of time to occur. *Quickly* the Galatians forsook the true gospel for a false one.[38] In the Revelation, John revealed that the church at Ephesus *quickly* lost its first love, only a few years after the Apostle Paul commended their love for one another in his epistle to them. The Corinthians *quickly* abandoned the teaching that Paul had espoused during his eighteen months with them.[39] Their quarreling, immorality, pride, and doctrine (salvation, baptism, Lord's Supper, resurrection) resulted in an ineffective and anemic church whose testimony was seriously degraded before the lost of Corinth. The process of decay can happen very quickly, but the processes of turning the situation around can take an enormous investment of time.

---

[37] Arnold L. Cook, *Historical Drift: Must My Church Die?* (Camp Hill, PN: Christian Publications, 2000), 10.

[38] C.f. Galatians 5:1.

[39] C.f. Acts 18:11.

Jesus on Revitalization

The Lord Jesus addressed a series of church revitalization issues in His rebukes and commendations to the Seven Churches of Asia Minor. Many of His teachings speak to the church's tendency to abandon (often quickly) the practices that He established. Jesus recognized the temptation to turn back to one's former manner of living. Jesus said, *No one, after putting his hand to the plow and looking back, is fit for the kingdom of God.* [40] Jesus clearly confronts the sins of commission in the churches of Ephesus, Pergamum, Sardis, and Laodicea and commands them to repent.[41] He tells the wicked Jezebel, and those who follow her in the church at Thyatira, to repent.[42] One could encapsulate the work of church revitalization in Jesus' charge to Sardis, *Wake up, and strengthen the things that remain, which were about to die; for I have not found your deeds completed in the sight of My God.*[43]

The Causes of Struggle in the Church

The New Testament addresses the situation of the struggling church from one of two distinct perspectives; their struggles stem either from sin or from opposition. The New Testament presents no

---

[40] Luke 9:62.

[41] C.f. Revelation 2:5, 16; 3:5, 19.

[42] Revelation 2:21-22.

[43] Revelation 3:2.

other cause of church struggle. The sins that cause the stagnation of the church can take two forms, sins of omission and sins of commission. Jesus definitely spoke to both situations.

The Sin of Omission

Jesus addressed both forms of sin in the Gospels and in the Letters to the Seven Churches. Jesus' teaching on prayer is the clearest on the sin of omission. He taught His disciples to pray at all times and not lose heart. His closest disciples failed miserably during the Lord's agony in the Garden of Gethsemane by preferring sleep to prayer. Modern disciples are no more faithful than the ones Jesus had with Him in the garden. The prayerlessness of God's people is not surprising, given the condition of the church. The lack of prayer reveals the priority of God in the believers' lives. "Before it is anything else, lack of prayer is a lack of hunger for God."[7] The lack of fervent prayer is contributory to the stagnation of the church. Prayerlessness is one of the barriers to church revitalization. If churches are going to be renewed, they must rediscover the intimacy with God that prayer affords.

The Sin of Commission

Jesus rebukes the churches of Asia Minor, except Smyrna and Philadelphia – these He exhorts to persevere in their difficult circumstances as they struggled against persecution in the form of opposition, resulting from sin. In His admonition to the church at Ephesus, Jesus revealed a serious barrier to church revitalization – their failure to address and to repent of their sin. Jesus threatened to remove the lampstand from the church at Ephesus, unless they repent.[44]

Opposition to the Church Itself

In the Book of Acts there was Roman and Jewish opposition, meaning the church experienced both civil and religious persecution. In the Book of Galatians, the Judaizers within the church were intense legalists, rule-makers, and watchdogs. In the community of Ephesus there was opposition from those in the synagogue. In Asia Minor there were many who opposed the church, including the Nicolaitans, the synagogue of Satan, those who hold to Balaam's teaching, and those who tolerate Jezebel's teaching. The solution for opposition to the church is prayer.

Opposition to Pastoral Leadership

In scripture, there was more opposition to the pastoral leadership than to the church itself! In Paphos, Elymas the magician opposed the churches leadership. In Syrian Antioch, Peter and the Jews from Jerusalem opposed the churches leadership stance from the Jerusalem Conference. In Jerusalem, Pisidian Antioch, Iconium, Berea, Thessalonica, Lystra and Derbe the Jews opposed the church's leadership. In Philippi, the masters of the slave girl

---

[44] Revelation 2:5.

opposed the church's leadership. In Corinth, there was opposition from the critics of Paul's apostleship. Lastly, even in Ephesus there was opposition from the synagogue Jews, Jewish exorcists, Demetrius and the silversmiths. Pastoral leaders withstand their opposition with prayer and with perseverance.

Jude Addresses Revitalization

The need for strengthening the church is apparent in the Epistle of Jude, in which Jude, the half-brother of the Lord Jesus, exhorts the general audience of the faithful to *"contend earnestly for the faith"* against the false teachers. The false teachers were guilty of three heinous sins: Perverting the gospel, engaging in sexual misconduct, and rejecting spiritual authorities. They were seriously damaging the testimony of the church because these false teachers were engaged in licentiousness, the disregarding of sexual restraints and denying the Lord Jesus Christ. They impeded the functionality of the church because they rejected spiritual authorities. Their personal, mystical experiences overrode the spiritual authorities; they viewed their own dreams as authoritative revelation. They were grumbling faultfinders and arrogant people-flatterers, seeking their own advantage.

The Book of Hebrews Reveals a Declining Church

The Jewish converts to Christianity were having a difficult time holding on their faith. The Hebrew church was a long-established church. We know this because the author of Hebrews expects that some of the his recipients should have become teachers by the time he wrote the letter, but their spiritual growth was thwarted, if not lost all together, because they needed to be taught the elemental principles of Christianity all over again.[45] Actual eyewitnesses to the resurrection had testified to them, and the Hebrew church had witnessed the manifesting work of the Holy Spirit in signs, wonders, miracles, and spiritual gifts,[46] yet they still drifted.[47] The church had some great examples to follow, excellent examples of faith and practice.[48] The church had experienced some persecution. They became public spectacles through "reproaches and tribulations," but their faith allowed them to stand their ground and not give up.[49] Their suffering was not very severe however, because the writer reminded them that they had not yet resisted to the point of shedding of blood in their striving against sin, but they had forgotten the Lord's exhortation that some suffering accompanied their discipline as sons from their loving Heavenly Father.[50] The writer of Hebrews seems to ask, 'If you did not give up in the past when you were persecuted, why are you giving up so easily now?'

---

[45] Hebrews 5:12.

[46] Hebrews 2:3-4.

[47] Hebrews 2:1.

[48] Hebrews 13:7.

[49] Hebrews 10:32-33.

[50] Hebrews 12:4-5.

Paul the Church Revitalizer

Paul had long been a revitalizer. Even before he trusted Jesus as Savior and Lord, he was revitalizing Judaism from what he believed was false doctrine in the teaching of those who followed *The Way*. Paul was the model Jew, circumcised on the eighth day, of the nation of Israel, of the tribe of Benjamin, a Hebrew of Hebrews. He was trained as a Pharisee under Gamaliel, a leading rabbi of his time, and by Paul's own admission, was zealously persecuting the scourge of Christianity that he believed threatened Judaism.[51] He persecuted *The Way* by arresting and imprisoning men and women, and he expressed his hearty approval when they were put to death.[52]

The first recorded ministry of Paul was to deliver a contribution to the famine-stricken church in Jerusalem from the Antioch church.[53] Paul was not included as a speaker at the Jerusalem Conference, according to the Acts. However, the apostles and elders there trusted Paul and Barnabas to deliver a letter with the results of the Conference to the dispersed churches in Antioch, Syria, and Cilicia.[54] Paul was certainly concerned for the churches that he

---

[51] Philippians 3:5-6.

[52] C.f. Acts 7:58-8:1; 22:3-5; 26:10-11.

[53] Acts 11:29-30.

[54] Acts 15:22-23.

helped to establish during his First Missionary Journey. Scripture explicitly states that the reason for the Second Missionary Journey was to return to the churches that he established in order to check on their health and progress.[55] The mission to strengthen the churches was successful.[56] The Third Missionary Journey had the same purpose – to strengthen the churches.[57] At some point, and again Acts gives no record of this even, Paul leaves young Titus behind on Cyprus to strengthen the churches. Paul left Titus there to organize the churches' leadership.[58] Paul sends another young protégé, Timothy, to Thessalonica to strengthen the church's faith and to encourage their continuation in the faith. Paul was forced to leave Thessalonica after three Sabbaths due to persecution.[59]

Paul wrote letters to the churches and his protégés Timothy and Titus about revitalization and demonstrated it practically through service. He had a missionary heart and a revitalizer passion. For Paul, the Great Commission was not just a ministry to unreached people and places; it was also a ministry of

---

[55] Acts 15:36, 41.

[56] Acts 16:5.

[57] Acts 18:23.

[58] C.f. Titus 1:5.

[59] 1Thessalonians 3:2; cf. Acts 17:1-10.

renewal and revitalization.[60]

The Old Testament is Replete with Examples of Revitalization

The speaking prophets of the Northern and Southern Kingdoms were cognizant of their nation's sins and were attempting revitalization. Jeremiah was deeply concerned about the destruction of Jerusalem. He prophesied that no one would have pity on Jerusalem or ever mourn for her.[61] He poetically added that even the roads leading to Zion would mourn because they would be devoid of worshippers.[62] A few kings of the South were excellent reformers (Asa, Jehoshaphat, Uzziah, Hezekiah, and Josiah). Sadly, their reforms had varying degrees of effectiveness and few of their reforms outlived their reigns. The few reforms of the Northern Kingdom came, not from the monarchy, but from the people.[63]

Ichabod, the Glory Departed

God manifested His glorious presence as He led

---

[60] Harry Lloyd Reeder, III, "The Ministry of Revitalization: 'Embers to a Flame'" (PhD diss., Reformed Theological Seminary, Charlotte, NC, 2002), 36.

[61] Jeremiah 15:5.

[62] C.f. Lamentations 1:4.

[63] 2 Chronicles 31:1.

the people of Israel out of Egypt, visible in a pillar of cloud by day and a pillar of fire by night. Just before God gave Moses the Ten Commandments on Mount Horeb, He told Moses that an angel would lead them into the Land of Promise. God Himself threatened that He would no longer go with them for Israel was an obstinate people.[64] God later rescinded this threat because of Moses' intercession and even allowed Moses to see His glory after Moses begged to see it. Some scholars have suggested that this was simply a rhetorical effect by God to get Israel's attention.[65] Rhetorical effect or genuine threat, it was a traumatic day for Moses and all of Israel. That day they came very close to seeing the glory of the Lord depart from them. The glory of God came down and filled the newly constructed Tabernacle,[66] and later the Temple in Jerusalem built by Solomon.[67] Once again, the Jews proved to be an obstinate people who committed idolatry and practiced injustice, so the presence of God left the Jerusalem Temple prior to its looting and destruction by the Babylonians. Ezekiel saw a vision of God's glory departing the Temple in Ezekiel 9-10, and the city burned in judgment as His presence left. God's glory and power can depart in subtle ways as

---

[64] Exodus 33:2-6.

[65] Douglas K. Stuart, vol. 2, *Exodus*, The New American Commentary (Nashville: Broadman & Holman Publishers, 2006), 690.

[66] Exodus 40.

[67] 2 Chronicles 7.

well. The glory of God can depart and a sinful person may not even notice the glory departed. In one of the saddest verses in the Bible, the Nazarite judge Samson did not even realize that the glorious presence of the Lord had left him after his hair was cut.[68] Could the contemporary church be just as oblivious to the departed glory and power of God? I argue that this is exactly the case. In the final days of the period of the Judges, the Philistines came against Israel in battle at Aphek. The Philistines oppressed Israel and slew 4,000 Israelites. The Israelites brought up the Ark of the Covenant for their next engagement. This time, they used the Ark as a talisman to ensure victory; they found nothing but defeat again and lost an additional 30,000 lives, including the two sons of the High Priest Eli, Hophni and Phineas.[69] Even worse, the Philistines captured the Ark of the Covenant, the very symbol of God's presence, from the nation of Israel. The sad news of the "great slaughter" and the capture of the Ark caused Eli to fall backward from his seat, break his neck, and die. The same news caused the wife of Phineas to go into immediate labor.[70] She gave birth to a son and died, and in this dark time for her and for her nation, her son was given the name *Ichabod* (the glory departed).[71] Could the glory of God have

---

[68] Judges 16:20.

[69] 1 Samuel 4:10.

[70] 1 Samuel 4:17-19.

[71] 1 Samuel 4:19-22.

departed from this generation because of the sins of the nation and of His church?

An Exilic Period Example

In one vision of Ezekiel, in a nondescript valley, a multitude of disconnected, dry bones, representing the scattered people of Israel, lay on the ground. After the fall of Jerusalem, Judah was scattered and dispirited. Scripture omits exactly who they were and how they died. God made the prophet walk all around the valley and through the midst of the bones to see the deadness. Perhaps to test the son of man or to pique Ezekiel's curiosity, God asked, *Can these bones live?*[72] Ezekiel knew that humanly speaking it was impossible, so his answer was somewhat guarded that only the Lord God knew that answer. By God's Spirit, they live again. They stood up a vast army.

The Post-Exilic Period

Nehemiah rebuilds the walls of Jerusalem. He was the most unlikely person for the task, a mere cupbearer. Some Septuagint manuscripts say he was a eunuch, yet the Hebrew text does not reflect this. Had Nehemiah's opponents known of his emasculation, they would have used this information to disqualify him from leadership because scripture did not permit a eunuch into the congregation of Israel. Second Maccabees describes "Neemias" performing priestly duties. If that were so, he would

---

[72] Ezekiel 37:3.

have been a Levite, however, nothing in the authoritative text suggests he was from the tribe of Levi. Nehemiah certainly possessed holiness, wisdom, intelligence (he had to be well-educated and multi-lingual), and passion. Nehemiah heard about the desperate situation of the Jerusalemites and that they were a reproach. He was broken by the news and he prayed for a man so well known for his *actions*, Nehemiah spent a great deal of time *being still* in prayer before the Lord. Nehemiah also confessed. Confession is often the prerequisite before the Lord will bless his people.

Revitalization is the work leaders do to ensure that the conditions of God are met for revival and in order that the people of God are prepared when the Sovereign God begins to move. The process of church revitalization is more than a recipe a leader follows. Every church, field, and circumstance is different. Churches that experience prolonged stagnation, plateau, or decline are generally those that have lost the passion to see their church influence the lives of the people in the community around them for the cause of Christ. The way out of their circumstances and back to a healthy life and ministry is very individualistic. Much has been written about the process of revitalization, most of which concentrates upon the human effort needed to see the change. Change is the operative word. The authority structure, ministry model, and philosophy of ministry may need to change, but in reality, what needs to change is the church's heart. The church cannot and will not produce the lasting fruit God desires, unless the church repents and God breathes once again upon His church. Someone has to begin the process of revitalization. It was the lowly cupbearer Nehemiah, who had a passion to rebuild a city, to restore a nation, and to lead the people from being a reproach to the name of God.

CHAPTER 4
Building Momentum for Church Revitalization

While leading RenovateConference.org, I have noticed that the race is about to begin! You are waiting at the starting line for the starter's horn to sound and the sailing race to commence. The timer's clock shows there is still twenty minutes to go before the race horn sounds. It's going to be a while, that much you know as you look around, because most of the boats are still at a dead stop. But with less than ten minutes to go before the start there is a new wave of activity beginning around you. The race participants display well-rehearsed activity and the sails fill with air as they begin to move towards the starting line. Some start fast and others start out ever so slowly. It seems to take the larger boats so long to get going!

When younger I raced sailboats of all sizes. It was so easy to get a 14 foot *Hobbie Cat* moving as compared to the 69 foot *Morgan Out-Islander* deep hull. But once that larger sailboat began to move the wind within its sails it had no problem maintaining full speed and plowing through the water with great efficiency!

It's the principle of inertia at work: things at rest tend to want to stay at rest and things in motion tend to want to stay in motion.

That is also true in church revitalization efforts:

Sometimes the greatest risk is in doing nothing.

The inertia that a moving object builds up is called momentum. It takes lots of energy to build up momentum, but it takes far less energy to maintain it. Momentum is more than a principle of physics. It is a principle we can apply to our personal lives and to the life of a renewing church as well. Momentum in church revitalization efforts will out distance negative skunking every time.

Have you met any *Church Skunkers* in your church revitalization efforts? Church skunking is the ploy that happens frequently within local church renewal efforts, when pessimistic church members spray negativity all over those creative church members who are trying to spark the renewal efforts of the church. A well-known example would be the tried-but-true expression by skunkers "We tried that years ago and it did not work."

When you have the power of momentum, the skunkers will try hard to slow things down, but keeping the energy moving forward is vital to a church's renewal efforts. Let us look at the importance of momentum in a church's revitalization strategy:

The Muscle of Momentum

First an illustration: Two teams have a game together. The team the experts consider to be the underdog has previously played teams not as good as they are, so they've won all of their games and they're undefeated. The better team has played teams ranked as better than themselves, so they've lost all their games. Who's going to win? No one can know for certain, but a betting person would be smart to put money on the underdog team that's undefeated. Momentum can be a big advantage!

John Maxwell, a nationally-known church leadership expert, has written a book called *The 21 Irrefutable Laws of Leadership*. One of the 21 laws is the law of momentum. Maxwell argues that a leader must create and sustain momentum among those he leads if he is to succeed.[73] Someone has well said: A minister doesn't become truly effective as a leader until after seven years at a church.

Even revitalizing churches can experience a lack of momentum when there are few things to measure relative to growth, either spiritually or numerically during the initial renewal stage. The church has been on a plateau for a portion of time and deciding to begin an effort to revitalize the church is often more of a wish than a desire to make the necessary decisions that will bring about renewed vision. This inertia of going nowhere does not last long, however. Negative momentum (going backward faster and faster) begins if an aggressive drive for life is not pursued.

Jesus Told a Story about Momentum

Momentum played a role in one of the stories

---

[73] Thomas Nelson Publisher, Nashville, TN. 1998.

Jesus told. The story is about a wealthy man who had to be away on business for an extended period of time. He called together his three associates and gave them his wealth to invest while he was gone. One was given five talents, another was given two, and the third was given one talent to oversee.

A talent was about what an ordinary worker could earn in 20 years. For comparison, let's use $30,000 for a worker's annual salary today. That is easy math for us to work with. That means one worker was given $3 million, another $1.2 million, and the third $600,000.

After a long period of time the wealthy man returned and found that the first associate had invested the $3 million and doubled it to $6 million. The second associate had invested his as well, and also doubled it—to $2.4 million. The third, however, had simply hid his $600,000 in a mattress, a tin can in the backyard, or some place like that, and had the same $600,000 to give back to his boss.

The boss was very pleased with the first two men for doubling his money, but he was angry with the third man. He took the $600,000 he had given to that man and gave it to the one with $6 million. Jesus wants His followers to see the importance of using whatever God gives us in life. We're to invest wisely what He's given us in opportunities, finances, abilities, and time. Jesus indicates that when we attempt to do something with what we've been given, we're going to end up with more, and this increase will increase even more. In Jesus' story, the man who had acquired the ten talents was given an eleventh (the one taken from the man who did nothing) presumably to continue to multiply his boss's wealth.

Jesus summarized the story by saying, "For everyone who has will be given more, and he will have abundance. Whoever does not have, even what he has will be taken from him" (Matthew 25:29). That's the principle of momentum at work. The one who works and takes risks to multiply what he has been given by God has even more, and the one who doesn't do anything to gain more will lose what he has. Sometimes the greatest risk is in doing nothing.

Some things that Cause Us to Lose Momentum

There are many things that cause us to lose our momentum in Church Revitalization.

- Discouragement can cause us to lose our momentum in Church Revitalization
- Failure can cause us to lose our momentum in Church Revitalization
- A lack of focus can cause us to lose our momentum in Church Revitalization
- Ungratefulness can cause us to lose our momentum in Church Revitalization
- Inattention can cause us to lose our momentum in Church Revitalization

These are all part of the factors that can cause

resistance to our forward momentum in church revitalization!

Positive experiences and memories of the past can either hamper or build momentum in Church Revitalization.

I heard about one couple who ran out of gas while traveling. It happened at an exit ramp, at the top of which was a gas station. The husband figured he could push the car up the ramp to the station, so he told his wife to get behind the steering wheel. He leaned into the back bumper with his shoulder, and pushed and pushed. It was really hard work, but eventually he pushed the car up to the pump at the gas station.

"Wow! That hill was steeper than I thought," he breathlessly told his wife.

"I know," she replied. "It was so steep I thought we might roll backward and I'd run you over, so I kept the brakes on."

You can add fear to the list of things that keep us from building momentum in Church Revitalization!

Intentional Steps toward Building Momentum in Church Revitalization

There are several steps we can take to build momentum in revitalization:

Understand it takes time and persistence to

renew a church!

Jesus said God's kingdom grows in influence like yeast does in bread dough.[74] Who wants to sit and watch bread rise? Get a life! Bread rises really slowly, but it does happen! Reversing negative momentum, or getting positive momentum going from a dead stop, takes time and persistence.

I have observed as a pastor how an individual losing a mate is a life-wrenching event. The first year is often one in which the widow or widower makes little progress at rebuilding a life. Some remain immobilized for the remainder of their lives. There are those, however, who begin to join life again by little steps: starting back to church, visiting a friend in the hospital, or joining in the celebrations of the holidays and special family events once again.

Revitalizing churches gain momentum slowly as well. A church's small group ministry, missions, lay leadership development, and other key areas of church life also seemed to take a long time before there is significant growth. Research has shown that a minister does not become truly effective as a leader until after seven years at any particular church.

Revitalizing churches are not well served when there is a change of pastoral leadership every three or four years. Momentum in a church revitalization effort takes time to build.

---

[74] C.f. Matthew 13:33; Luke 13:20.

Just do something—almost anything.

Doing nothing will not change anything; in fact, it usually makes things worse. In Jesus' story of the three men given the talents, the criticism of the man with one talent was that he did nothing. We can begin by just doing a little something, being obedient to God in little ways. After all, most of life's greatest achievements are made up of small things.

Building positive momentum in a revitalizing church involves identifying small and manageable goals that, with prayer and some effort, can be achieved. It requires moving beyond the momentum-killing idea that "We've never done it that way before."

Build on Your Successes

Focus on your latest forward progress. Many of the Psalms were written by people in trouble who reviewed the ways God had helped them in the past. This gave them the confidence to move forward and seize the future, and their psalms usually end on that confident note. One word of warning! Even those positive experiences and memories can either hamper or build momentum. A nostalgic wishing list can hurt even a church in the midst of successful renewal! Do not get buried in such but remember, God is the giver of good gifts.

Work on the serendipitous breakthroughs for church revitalization.

Albert Einstein realized what more revitalization leaders need to discern: that a major breakthrough can launch a church from good to great, so great church revitalizers always press for that breakthrough. Revitalization breakthroughs occur when we continually:

1. Meet the needs of the community (which allows us to stay in the playing field);

2. Improve ourselves and our church revitalization assistance team; and

3. Succeed. It's a fact that there is no success like success.

Pushing for a revitalization breakthrough generates what John Maxwell describes as a leader's best friend - momentum. Momentum makes your work or your mission easier to accomplish than anything else. While attending his training events I would often hear John say:

> Momentum is worth three staff members. In fact, if some leaders would get rid of the right three staff members, they might instantly get some momentum.

When you have no momentum, things look worse than they really are. And when you have momentum, it makes things look better than they ever seemed to be. So you've got to push for the breakthrough in church revitalization. A revitalization effort must move from build-up to breakthrough, from good to great. Good is build-up; great is breakthrough.

But there is a temptation that comes with a breakthrough in church revitalization and the momentum that comes with it. The temptation is to ease up and celebrate the initial victory. You just kind of want to sit back and say, "Wow! Aren't we good?" It just feels good to know you have achieved something even a little something. And while it is OK to celebrate, we have to remember that the next play just might get us beat. Once you have that ball rolling, the compounding effect is so huge you don't ever want that ball to stop.

What do you do when the momentum stalls?

The time to ease up is when things have slowed down, when you do not have momentum and when you do not have a breakthrough. When the church revitalization train already has stopped - get off and take a rest. You were not going anywhere anyway! But once the train gets going again, don't get off. When you have momentum and the breakthrough, it is dangerous to jump off. You could hurt yourself. You could hurt your church revitalization efforts.

So if you want to go from good efforts to great achievements in Church Revitalization, keep pushing toward a breakthrough. And when the church renewal momentum arrives, either because you are near the goal or because you have broken through, do not ease up. That is when you put the pedal to the metal.

Nine Ways to Create Momentum for Church Revitalization

Legendary football coach Paul 'Bear' Bryant said, "Have a plan. Follow the plan, and you'll be surprised how successful you can be. Most people don't have a plan. That's why it's is easy to beat most folks." In a recent survey, it was revealed that 79% of churches have little to no plans for outreach. This may be the reason why 85-90% of the churches in America are either plateaued or declining. Designing, executing and implementing outreach plans and strategies is one of the skills that pastors need to create positive momentum in their church's renewal efforts.

Here are a couple of insights that you can apply in planning your church revitalization strategies:

1. Develop a Church Revitalization Assistance Team (CRAT).

Too many church revitalizers try to carry the burden all by themselves, which is an unbiblical notion. Church revitalization is a team activity. Team building is one of the skills successful church revitalizers need in their tool belts. Learning to pick the right individuals on your church revitalization assistance team is essential. Guiding and leading the CRAT is imperative. Trusting the CRAT to implement the plan is empowering. Celebrating and encouraging the CRAT is imperative. I encourage church revitalizers to use short-term task groups with a specific task along with a starting and ending point. If you build a group for each of your major church revitalization initiatives your team building skills would improve each time. Team building is a skill which is honed through the "learning by doing" process. More will be said about how to build such a group later on in this book.

Remember in your church revitalization journey that getting key influencers involved in the renewal process is key to building positive momentum.

2. Develop a revitalization time line utilizing the rule of the ninety-day push.

To develop a good time line, start with the last date of the project and work backwards. This is what I call the "Law of the Ninety Day Push", which is to begin the detailed planning process at least three months before launch of the renewal effort. Most churches working in renewal can assume only three pushes a year with each one taking ninety days to accomplish. Then there is a much-needed time of rest for thirty days before you begin the next ninety-day charge.

3. The CRAT should brainstorm ideas for delivering strong biblical content that addresses the heart language issues of your mission field.

Many church revitalizers struggle with the creative aspects of leading revitalization. I suggest that church revitalizers research and purchase many of the good church revitalization tools available. Many of these come with time lines, job descriptions, graphics, sermon ideas and small group materials. The key is planning ahead. After the church has done a few of these campaigns, then they can take a shot at developing their own.

4. Raise the spiritual temperature of the church renewal efforts.

It is a must to incorporate a church-wide prayer project before and during the church revitalization effort. One example: Call the church to "pray for five neighbors, for five minutes a day, for five weeks" before the church revitalization effort. Another idea would be to mobilize the church to prayer walk your whole community before the church revitalization effort. You could also call the church to a season of prayer and fasting.

5. The CRAT should brainstorm ideas for creating buzz throughout the church and throughout the community.

Work with your Church Revitalization Assistance Team in thinking of ways to get the word out about your efforts towards renewal.

6. Drive the church revitalization theme throughout the church.

Creating a sense of synergy throughout the church during renewal is important. Getting every section of the church moving in the same direction during church revitalization effort is a momentum building experience that creates positive energy and good morale. So take your revitalization theme and drive it throughout the church from the silver haired seniors to energetic youth, from your innovating singles to your toddlers!

7. Develop church revitalization comeback events.

Creating opportunities for new guests to connect relationally, as well as spiritually, is crucial to having a successful church revitalization journey. Planning some type of family friendly event is a great way to get people involved in serving for the first time and connecting relationally with others in the church. Offering entry level bible studies within weeks of your special events is important in providing those next steps for those that are spiritually interested. Finally, you want to offer people an opportunity to connect with the church and its leadership by offering some type of newcomer's luncheon or party at the church revitalizers event where they hear the story and vision of the church and its renewal strategy as well as connect relationally with key leaders. This is also a great time to offer those who have distanced themselves from the church the opportunity to return to the church. Though it is an oldie it is still a goodie, have a friend day in your church and work towards reconnecting with your memberships neighbors. I used a theme "Hey Neighbor, Let's Become Neighbors Again!" Creating some comeback activities is a good way to re-involve past members and participants with a vigorous new vision for the future.

8. Recruit volunteers to fill needed ministry roles.

Doing special events targeted towards church renewal and evangelism is a great chance to recruit new volunteers for various tasks in the renewal effort. Utilizing a new group of workers must be focused around what you are doing in revitalization and not on the continual undergirding of dying programs. A great idea is to develop new small groups and discover home hosts for these new groups.

9. Drive your newly developed missional values deeper into the changing culture of your church during the church revitalization efforts.

Remember, anytime you create a church revitalization event, it is an opportunity to drive your newly developed missional vision and values deeper into the lives of new and existing church participants. The values of evangelism, community, spiritual dependence and community transformation come alive during the church revitalization journey and provide opportunities for personal growth and corporate spiritual maturity.

Remember the Muscle of Momentum.

It takes a great deal of energy to get a yacht moving across the water, but once it gets going its nearly unstoppable! That is the muscle of momentum in church revitalization. The little play craft is able to get moving more quickly but the larger yacht is able to stand up to the rough seas while the smaller craft is thrown about by turbulence. Momentum helps you with assimilating new people into the life of renewal work. Momentum allows you to grow past levels that might otherwise stall your revitalization efforts. Momentum helps you create more momentum. Momentum is that little extra that allows a revitalizing church to keep its focus on what is worthy and right for this hour without sinking at the most crucial time just at the beginning of the race. Church Revitalizers need to learn to harness the muscles of momentum and discover that they will greatly assist your revitalization in moving across the starting line of growing a revived church with God's leading.

Keep the wind in your sails and press on!

CHAPTER 5
The Biblical Qualification of a Church Revitalization Leader

Shortly after I began to work in the field in church revitalization, a pastor friend and I went to lunch together to discuss this important work. He asked me one of the most probing questions that I have ever been asked, "Why should anyone listen to you about church revitalization?" I was not offended by the question because I know my friend's heart. It was a direct and honest question. I gave him this earnest answer, "Honestly, I am not the best person to lead this effort, but I'm like the guy who sees a child drowning in a pool. In that situation, you don't seek out the most qualified lifeguard; you just jump into the pool and save the child." There are more qualified people out there, to be sure, but there is a need and here I am.

The qualifications to lead something like church revitalization are important – I truly believe that, but it has been said that God qualifies the called, he doesn't call the qualified. This aphorism sounds correct to our spiritual ears as we consider how God uses key individuals in scripture. Think about it, what qualifications did Noah have to build an enormous ark? What qualifications did Moses have to lead God's people out of bondage in Egypt? What qualifications did the farmer-shepherd Amos have to preach against the wickedness of Israel? What qualifications did the cup-bearer Nehemiah have in leading wall construction? The answer is quite simple – each of these leaders was commissioned by God for a great work that could only be accomplished as he trusted in the Lord.

Please do not hear me say that qualifications are unimportant because they are. Each of the people in the examples just mentioned possessed remarkable qualities of character, skill, wisdom, and faith. As we consider some qualities that are found in church revitalizers, see if these qualities are in you or can be developed in you. Here are a few, less-well-known qualities that are found in revitalizers that are substantiated by the revitalization leadership of Nehemiah:

Revitalization Leaders Possess Brokenness over the Situation before Them.

Hanani, Nehemiah's brother, brought news that Jerusalem was still in distress because the walls were still torn down and the gates were burned with fire. The people there were suffering and apparently nobody was helping them. This news should not have been a surprise to Nehemiah; the walls were destroyed and the gates burned some fifty years earlier. Ezra mentions a previous attempt to repair the wall.[75] Perhaps, Nehemiah was surprised because he had expected to hear about the wall's completion, instead he heard of its destruction. The news caused Nehemiah great despair, causing him to weep and mourn for days.[76] Revitalization starts with

---

[75] Ezra 4:12-23.

[76] Nehemiah 1:4.

brokenness.

Revitalization Leaders Seek God and Get Their Vision from Him.

Nehemiah was deeply moved when he heard the sad report about Jerusalem. For many days he mourned and prayed over the situation caused by the people's sins, including his own. Out of his awareness of the need and his immersion in prayer, Nehemiah developed the conviction that God's people, now returned to the holy land, must honor God and rebuild the city walls. As the vision formed, Nehemiah realized that he himself had been called to carry it out. Frequently those who form such a vision will be called by God to fulfill it. His calling came out of his vision! Awareness of need + Intense Prayer + Conviction + Vision = Calling.

Revitalization Leaders Need an Active, Effective and Consistent Prayer Life.

Nine individual prayers of Nehemiah are recorded in the book that bears his name. Nehemiah is well known as a man of action. He got things done – he rebuilt the walls of Jerusalem in only fifty-two days. He is known for cursing those who intermarried (against God's commands), slapping them and pulling their hair out for it, and making them swear never to do it again. He was a man of action, but do not overlook the quality of his prayer life. He prayed for God's forgiveness for the sins of Israel, his family, and especially his own sins. He never prayed for his enemies, but he prayed for God to fight for him when his enemies tried to interfere with his anointed purpose. Nehemiah prayed for success, strength, and that God would remember him for the good that he tried to do.[77]

Revitalization Leaders Are Completely Honest about Their Situations.

Nehemiah was honest with God about sin, about the corruption of his people, and about their failure to keep God's commandments, the statutes, and the ordinances. Nehemiah was honest with himself – he allowed his sadness to show to the king and even confessed that he was "very much afraid" to do so. Nehemiah was honest with the King and asked permission to go and to rebuild the city, giving King Artaxerxes a definite date that he would return, which he kept. Nehemiah was honest with the people. He told them what a bad situation they were in and how the hand of the Lord had been upon him. Nehemiah was even honest with his enemies (Sanballat, Tobiah, and Geshem). He reminds them that the God of Heaven would give the Israelites success, and that these enemies of God would have no portion, right, or memorial in Jerusalem. In other words, "God will help us to rebuild the wall, and you won't be invited to the party!"

Revitalization Leaders Are Patient Plodders Who Understand the Importance of Timing.

[77] C.f. Nehemiah 5:19, 13:14, 13:22, 13:3.

Nehemiah never enjoyed much fanfare during his life, nor was he ever accused of having a charismatic personality, but over time, he got big things done. As we say in Oklahoma, he wasn't a show pony, he was a plow horse! Nehemiah's lasting legacy was not the rebuilt walls because the Romans tore them down again and nothing of them remains today. Nehemiah's legacy was the hope that he gave to his people and the hope subsequent readers of his namesake book still receive when they use it as a model for revitalization. Perhaps Nehemiah knew, *He who keeps a royal command experiences no trouble, for a wise heart knows the proper time and procedure.*[78]

Revitalization Leaders Are Passionate People Who Are Completely Committed to Their Lord, the Church, and the Revitalization Process.

What Nehemiah lacked in construction expertise, he made up for in passion. We know that Nehemiah traveled 900 miles to lead the people of Jerusalem in the arduous task of rebuilding the walls around the city and repairing its gates. Nehemiah executed his plan to raise the entire wall simultaneously at forty-five different sites, including ten gates. Nehemiah planned his work, worked his plan, and trusted the results to God. Nehemiah was passionate about addressing the real problem, one that his brother reported at the beginning of the book, that the people of Jerusalem were in distress and were a reproach. The word *reproach* in Hebrew describes spiritual

---

[78] Ecclesiastes 5:8.

taunting. The enemies of Israel were taunting the people that their God was weak and uncaring, and that they were a disgrace to the name of their God. When the walls went up, so did the people's spirits! Nehemiah stood up to the enemies, rebuilt the walls, revitalized the people, and gave the people of Jerusalem a new security. They were never threatened by their enemies again in the book.

Church Revitalizers Are Hopeful and Not Just Optimistic

Church revitalizers are hopeful, and not just optimistic; there is a difference. Rabbi Jonathon Sacks says: "Optimism is the belief that things will get better. Hope is the faith that, together, we can make things better. Optimism is a passive virtue, hope an active one. It takes no courage to be an optimist, but it takes a great deal of courage to have hope."[79] Nehemiah was a hope dealer! God gave him hope in the midst of despair after hearing the awful news when he discovered that God's hand was upon him. He gave hope back to the distressed people of Jerusalem as he led them to rebuild their walls.

Church Revitalizers Inspire More Than They Motivate.

Nehemiah never intended to rebuild the wall as a monument to his own accomplishment, but rather to

---

[79] Jonathon Sacks, *The Dignity of Difference* (New York: Continuum Books, 2002, 2003), 206.

inspire and lead a dispirited and faithless people to accomplish something great. Nehemiah inspired them by relating how God had been at work in his own life. He knew the people would follow someone who had been with God. Perhaps the reproach of today's church will inspire someone to lead the church to greatness once again.

Church Revitalizers Are Able to Take Extraordinary Risks in order to Achieve Their Objectives.

Nehemiah had the passion and personal commitment to respond to his life's calling, despite numerous threats to his well-being. Nehemiah's life was in jeopardy when he asked leave from the king to rebuild the walls. During the construction of the wall, Nehemiah endured conflict in the form of mockery, slander, threats, taunts, attacks, ridicule, intimidation, temptation, attempts at discrediting him, and false accusations against him. Nehemiah refused to be intimidated; he armed the people and kept them working. He even dealt with dissent among his own people, as well as a shortage of food that threatened everything. Nehemiah overcame each of these threats by keeping the objective in view.

The qualifications in Nehemiah that made his work successful centered on his ability to put his trust in the Lord. He allowed his life to be broken in order that it could be used. Nehemiah was a broken man for a broken city. He listened to the heart of his God and resolutely went about his work, inspiring others to join in this noble work. In the same way, churches today need selfless, broken, passionate leaders who love the Lord's church to take on this great need in our day, so God's people will no longer be a disgrace.

CHAPTER 6
Determining the Composition of the Church Revitalization Assistance Team

While leading RenovateConference.org, I have noticed that when putting together the *Church Revitalization Assistance Team (CRAT)* one should always start with players who have the right stuff and then let it push out to the water's edge. You want a team that is quite able, well-led, and displays the right characteristics.

Nine Questions for Determining Your Readiness to Revitalize a Church

Some early questions should be considered when launching into any revitalization effort. How do you know if your church is ready to participate in Church Revitalization? Start with asking yourself these following nine questions. The more you and your church can answer these questions affirmatively, the more prepared you are to begin the church revitalization process.

1) Do you and your people have a burden for lost people and a willingness to see your church revitalized and become healthy?

2) Has a leader surfaced to lead out?

3) Has your congregation shown a willingness to step out in faith and try new things?

4) Do you have a vision for your city and region?

5) Is your congregation spiritually mature and able to discern God's movement?

6) Has your congregation practiced a generous spirit?

7) Are you willing to risk?

8) Does your congregation have a genuine kingdom mindset?

9) Are you willing to invest resources (people & finances) towards renewing your church?

The Characteristics of Key Revitalization Team Members

In the selection of team members do not just make an announcement in church and accept all of those who volunteer. You must, as the pastor, select the right team and not become bogged down by those who either do not want the church to be revitalized and choose to be part of the team to disrupt the effort. Also you must not allow some to serve on the team who are notorious in church for not doing anything significant. These two types of individuals will destroy any real chance you have to revitalize one's church. Choose your team carefully and wisely or you will regret the effort in the final analysis. Here are some characteristics that are key to the health of the church revitalization assistance team:

Collaboration

Members must be first *willing* to work together

and then build the *ability* to work together as a unified core and not as individual MVP's! When you fill your team with cooperative individuals who are committed to the goal of revitalizing one's church, you have a greater chance to see it come to fruition. Collaborators are your partners and teammates in the journey. They will be the ones who will encourage you and lift you up as you keep the throttle pressed forward and the pace of change continuing.

Dedication

If you cannot find individuals who possess the dedication for the renewal journey, do no place them on this team. Team members must be sold on the idea of revitalizing a church and be fully committed to the task. Placing people on the team will not convince them of the need to renew a work. You must have individuals who are willing to persevere in the process of turning around one's church. It is not a quick fix and it will take time. You must take the time, spend the time and endure the time it will take to bring about renewal to one's church. Loyalty to the process of revitalization and the particular church as it works hard to survive will be a key.

Evangelistic Fervor

To serve effectively on a church revitalization assistance team, individual members must believe in evangelism. If you have a group on the team that does not believe in the work of reaching the lost for Christ Jesus, they will impede every single effort to impact the culture you are trying to reach around the church.

Evangelistic thinkers will have the passion needed to build the Kingdom by renewing churches into healthy bodies once again. Going after the lost of one's community and reaching them for Christ is still a key to growing a church regardless if it is a plant, a healthy church, or a declining church that needs revitalization.

Optimism

The joy of the Lord is one's strength and nothing is more helpful to a church revitalizer building a team to assist in the revitalization effort than those who choose joy over depression regardless of the circumstances. Church revitalization is a challenging endeavor, so you do not want naysayers on your Church Revitalization Assistance Team. The best type of person to serve on this team are those people who can find the opportunity in every obstacle. They are optimistic about the cause and refuse to fuss and feud over nonessential matters. There will be an intense effort by the status quo to place as many like-minded individuals onto a team so they can control any effort on their terms. This only leads to even more decline, because some of those in the church wanting renewal eventually see the big picture and do not want anything to do with the church anymore, and leave because of this negativity towards change and renewal. In a church becoming renewed, there will be negative people who will look at the new effort as giving up something that they hold dear. Stagnation is the thing they love and where they find comfort. Yet such people cannot be allowed to come into this group, or you are sunk.

Faith

The Church Revitalization Assistance Team must be people of faith! They must be willing to believe God for the impossible. They must be able to embrace a vision of what a revitalized church looks like. They must be willing to look beyond what is seen into the unseen. That takes great faith. The Bible says: *Now faith is the assurance of things hoped for, the conviction of things not seen.*[80]

Everybody has faith in something, even the most diehard skeptic. The question is whether or not that faith is in the right place and of the right amount. The revitalization team must be made up of people who believe in God for the impossible. They must believe in the person and work of the Lord Jesus. Throughout the Gospels, Jesus himself calls people to have faith in God. Many who run from the work of revitalization will in the end hear from the savior, "Oh, you of little faith." We want this team to be faith-full and not faith-less. In Matthew's gospel, we are given five examples of little faith and an additional five examples of great faith. The difference could be summarized in these statements: Little faith is smothered by fear, while great faith is strengthened by boldness. Little faith pays attention on the material world, while great faith places one's emphases on the spiritual world. Little faith makes choices based on what is doable for individuals, while great faith makes decisions based on what is possible for God.

---

[80] Hebrews 11:1.

87

Church Revitalization Assistance Team Individual Member Gifts

As well as the afore-mentioned characteristics, there are some additional, specific gifts that you should see displayed by at least some members of your team. Not everyone needs all of these, but you should fill your team with individuals who at least possess some of these traits. It is wise to have at least one of each of these types of individuals on the team.

Strategic Thinking

You will need at least one strategic thinker on the team, someone who is adept at reasoning through a process. This person understands goals, objectives, plans, and strategic steps. Strategic thinkers typically ask penetrating questions. Someone has well-stated that: *Thinking strategically first makes strategic planning work.*

Done well, a strategic plan provides a beneficial concentration that invigorates and transfers the church's organizational structure toward its real mission of revitalizing the church. For the church revitalization effort you need the kind of strategic thinker who can:

1. foresee the needed shifts the church must make

2. think diagnostically of the circumstances in the church that must be addressed

3. translate the changing culture around the local church

4. do something and not be paralyzed by a lack of activity

5. align others to the cause of revitalization, and

6. become a life-long learner.

I am sure there are others as well, but these will do to start you thinking strategically about what needs to happen for revitalization to have the best possible chance for success.

Institutional Memory

A person with this trait is an historian-type individual who will help the church to avoid repeating mistakes. A long-tenured pastor or staff member is such a likely person. An individual who has been a positive long term member can help the revitalization not to repeat past mistakes by providing past historical information at the appropriate time, which could help newbies understand the past failures and take necessary actions to not repeat the past again.

Ministry Contribution

People who are active in the church's current ministries will contribute greatly to the team's effectiveness. Determine which groups would be most helpful and involve them as they are needed. Because they are already busy doing the work of ministry, include them only when necessary. Having a large attendance is not your goal, revitalizing the church is the goal.

Creative Thinker

Every church in need of revitalization would like to have a throng of creative thinkers, if it was not for the mess they cause for those stuck in outdated norms and functions. Creative thinkers are an asset to the *Church Revitalization Assistance Team*. Revitalizing a plateaued church is not a traditional endeavor. You will want people who see things a bit off center. I have learned from revitalizing churches that people of habit do not have the ability to see other things. These types of creative team members will stretch the rest of the team. Creative people force others to break free from the confines of conventional wisdom. They help the rest of the team to clearly see new options and think clearly about the choices they make. What is the difference between the words reactive and creative? Answer: It is how you arrange the letters. The same can be said about creative thinkers. They have the ability to rearrange the way we think for the betterment of the church.

During the days while Bill Gates led Microsoft, he realized that he did not have to know everything. He recognized that he had employees who did. But, he appreciated the importance of taking the time to learn what they knew and absorb their creative thinking. He took time to listen to their ideas. He took time to think, to ponder the direction of Microsoft. The one who leads the church revitalization effort must be willing to spend the time listening to the creative ones in the group as they help bring the church out of its doldrums. Here is a great exercise to stimulate innovation and creativity for anyone who is going to lead the church revitalization effort of a local church:

1. Read with pen and notebook in hand; jot down any idea that comes into your consciousness.

2. Keep a notebook by your bed and in your car where you can keep track of ideas.

3. Write one idea down on a piece of paper and brainstorm any thought that comes from it: how to accomplish the idea, what to do about the idea, where to use the idea, who can help you implement the idea, and any other thought that enters your mind.

4. Read a non-fiction book every week. Read magazines, journals, online articles, all the time.

5. Clip articles and place them in a folder of related articles or ideas. Periodically, glance through the folder.

6. Create "idea files" in most folders in your computer. Create an idea or to-do file in your email program. Add ideas as they come to you.

7. Take time to stare out your window (if your setting deserves attention), play with a desk toy, take a quiet walk.

8. Do any rote activity that allows thoughts to swirl through your mind.

9. Encourage your church revitalization assistance team to do all of the above and share ideas with each other at "think" or brainstorm sessions.

10. Schedule annual retreats or off-site meetings to plan and generate ideas.

11. Develop a church member idea box.

12. Schedule think weeks, think days, or think hours for yourself or your work group.

Thinking time and learning time are both critical to creativity and innovation. The old adage: "stop to smell the roses" is true for both your current ministry and your long-term ministry. Take time to plant and harvest the ideas that fuel your progress and success. Creative thinking reigns.

Leading the Revitalization Team

Who should lead the Church Revitalization Assistance Team (CRAT)? What is the operative team size? I suggest that five to seven individuals serve on the CRAT in order to accompany the Revitalization Leader. Here are some CRAT responsibilities which should be considered. A CRAT will be responsible for at least the following actions:

Identify and recruit intercessors who will pray for the revitalization project.

Communicate a biblical understanding of church revitalization to the congregation.

Develop a biblical understanding of the directive to become healthy again.

Create awareness of the process of change that awaits the congregation (A missional endeavor).

Clarify relationships and mutual expectations with denominational leaders and with the church attempting revitalization.

Create a timeline for the project and identify critical milestones.

These actions will help the church in the effort of renewal and keep you and your team on track.

CHAPTER 7
How to Revitalize the Church

God loves the local church, and it is His desire to see it grow. Every church concerned about growth must be committed to revitalization. While leading RenovateConference.org, I have learned that if you are a church leader and are not extremely devoted to the time required to achieve renewal and health, then another member ought to lead the process. Not every church that renews its fellowship and moves forward is led through that process by its lead minister. Yet this minister must be part of the revitalization assistance team and participate in training the laity for that work, regardless of who leads the effort.

An estimated 177,000 Protestant churches in America have an average attendance of less than 100. Research tells us that more than 80 percent of U.S. churches are plateaued or declining. With another 50 to 75 churches closing their doors every week, we soon realize the importance of revitalizing the local church. It is impossible to turn any local church around until a group of individuals within that congregation becomes so steadfastly involved in its ministry that they will surrender almost everything for the eternal good of that church. Accept the fact that revitalization is often painful and difficult. If you are serious about it, you must be willing to invest a minimum of 1,000-plus days in the effort to achieve lasting success.

All who work in church revitalization will need the encouragement in these verses:

Love suffers long and is kind; love does not envy; love does not parade itself, is not puffed up; does not behave rudely, does not seek its own, is not provoked, thinks no evil; does not rejoice in iniquity, but rejoices in the truth; bears all things, believes all things, hopes all things, endures all things (1 Corinthians 13:4-7).

Beyond acting in love, the revitalization leader must be willing to make the necessary changes in ministry style to help the church revitalize.

Skills and Traits

While teaching on this subject in Kansas City recently, we considered some of the vital skills and traits necessary for pastors or church leaders when working in church renewal.

Prayer

Too many leaders ignore prayer in their personal lives, as well as in leading the church to be a people of prayer. Personal prayer and drawing other prayer warriors around you is vital to renewal! Only prayer can confront the reality of original sin in the church, through the Holy Spirit's guidance.

Spiritual Authenticity

A shoot-from-the-hip type leader can lead a new plant or go to some church and pull out his bag of tricks all over again. It is entirely different for a revitalization leader to stay with a difficult mission and see it through to the best days of that church's life. A shoot-from-the-hip style doesn't make a strong leader for church revitalization.

Enabler/Encourager

Realize that the goal is not to win all the battles but to enable a congregation, as much as possible, to move as one into its new future. The enabler has that wonderful gift of getting a church working together again.

Initiator/Energizer

The initiator demonstrates that it is a new day for the church and that victory can be achieved. He and the energizer can bring people together by creating "nudge" activities. Nudges are those little things that eventually build upon one another to create big things for church revitalization. Here is a brief Nudge List to help you understand the idea of creating activities which will have a positive impact on the congregation and those who can accomplish the specific task. These activities have been used to nudge a church into renewal:

1. Facility improvement (a little paint, rearranging the mess, cleaning up, etc.)

2. The pastor sharing his dreams for the church

3. Disciple-making and discipleship opportunities

4. A new music team

5. Visiting every member and prospect

6. Practical evangelism through community events

7. Creating a new members class

Facilitator/Catalyst

Give people some tools, then get out of the way and watch God work! The facilitator/catalyst does not look for plug-and-play solutions (programs), but looks for ideas that will work in his setting. Begin asking God for guidance, instead of asking Him to bless your ideas only after you have thought it all out.

Transformational Leader

Momentous church troubles may be faced and overcome by a single confident, unrelenting leader. The best solution to a predicament or a long-term issue that threatens any church is understanding the issue and its need for a change agent.[81] This leader has the ability to anticipate resistance and sabotage. He can tell the difference between the stuff people are arguing about and the emotional reality of the case.

---

[81] For more on this subject see: Cheyney, Tom. *The Church Revitalizer as Change Agent*, Orlando: Renovate Publishing Group, 2015.

Coach for Success

Teach the importance of persistence and remaining calm in the midst of turmoil. The ability to stay connected with everyone during these hard times is part of coaching your congregation for success. Members are watching you and your ability (or lack of it) to be an anxiety shock absorber and to display healthy emotional Teflon as you lead the church through the course of revitalization.

Manager/Director

Think about ideas and ways that will send a message to the community that you are doing something new. How can you share the dream using short-term, mid-term, and long-range ideas and goals for renewal? Remember, however, not to force things. Impatient revitalization leaders push too hard and seek quick fixes over steady wins.

Growth/Ambassador

Numerical growth is the least certain mark of church revitalization, yet the local church is not renewed without some numerical growth. The leader must be intentional about growth and health; these do not come by accident. Revitalized churches begin with a spiritually revitalized laity. If growth is measured in people getting involved in church ministries, then ministry must be made simple and the ministry teams easy to join.

Caregiver

Hurting people are not healthy people. Unhealthy people make for an unhealthy church. We need to bring people to health before we can begin to renew the church. Caregivers are wired in ways that will assist you in working toward health. They are glue that keeps your participants together and engaged.

Partner/Friend

Revitalization begins with you, the lead pastor. Learn from others early and often. A pastor must earn love and respect before he earns the right to lead in renewal. Be the congregation's friend and partner. It is difficulty for laity in the church to connect with and know how to support a pastor who is reclusive.

Visionary

Leading through the change needed to un-stick a stuck church is part of the visionary revitalization. Communicate early and often how renewal will take place and be implemented. Prepare yourself spiritually as the visionary and prepare your leaders spiritually. Then begin preparing your church spiritually.

Seek God's Guidance and Power

Church revitalization is not about finding the "magic pill" or "sure to succeed" program. It is about discovering God's vision for the church and practicing it! Instead of forcing your vision, help members discover their own for the local church.

Personal Commitment

To succeed in revitalization, the church must stop allowing a vocal minority to dictate what the church will or will not do. Utilize your caregivers to help keep the place firmly connected and glued as one. Everything that must be done in revitalization cannot happen in two or three hours on Saturday! We must change and grow as individuals if the church is going to change and grow. And in the end, God will receive the glory, not us.

CHAPTER 8
Welcome to the Passive Aggressive Church:
Advice to the Long-Tenured Church Revitalizer

While leading ChurchRevitalizer.com I have noticed a significant issue, in that the contemporary church experiences today often displays a passive aggressive tendency in dealing with conflict. The NYU Medical Center defines a passive aggressive individual as someone who "may appear to comply or act appropriately, but actually behaves negatively and passively resists." Passive aggressive people are generally unreasonable, are difficult to correct because they rarely express their hostility directly, and they repeat their behavior over time.[82]

Unfortunately, this behavior has found its way into the church. Rather than believers sitting down together to reconcile differences honestly, calmly, and biblically, they often act out in ways to get noticed or to make a statement. We should not be surprised at this; it reflects the practice of our culture where overt confrontation and any expression of hostility are discouraged. Coupled with today's politically correct environment, people do not, and often cannot, express their hurts and frustrations. Our schools and workplaces are programming people to address their problems institutionally, rather than personally, through processes rather than in person. Often

---

[82] Preston Ni, *Psychology Today*, "How to Spot and Deal With Passive-Aggressive People: 8 Keys to Surviving Passive-Aggressives at Home and at Work," January 5, 2014.

resolution never occurs. Their anger is pent up and eventually comes out. Sadly, this has led to violence in the workplace and in the school yard, and even the church. In fact, since 1999, 427 people have been killed by deadly force while participating in a place of worship; and more people have been killed in Southern Baptist churches than in any other denomination.[83]

Thankfully, not every disagreement will end in violence, but the vast majority of violent acts begin as a simple unresolved disagreement. If you think this is unique to our day and time, think again. James, the half-brother of Jesus, explained the source of this conflict to the recipients of his letter, *"What is the source of quarrels and conflicts among you? Is not the source your pleasures that wage war in your members? You lust and do not have; so you commit murder. You are envious and cannot obtain; so you fight and quarrel."*[84] He mentions quarrels, conflicts, war, and even murder! These occur because of lust, which is selfish, sinful desire that leads to revolt.[85] I am glad that violent acts are rare in churches, but I am disappointed to see passive aggressive activities in the life of believers who should know better.

---

[83] David Roach, *SBC Life: Journal of the Southern Baptist Convention*, "Protecting Your Church Against Violence," March 2013 issue.

[84] James 4:1-2.

[85] C.f. Galatians 5:17.

Passive aggressive behavior directed toward those in ministry seems to be on the rise as well. Yesterday I received a telephone call from a pastor friend. During the course of our conversation he shared about a woman in his church who obviously is upset with him. Every week, as he rises to preach, she picks up her personal effects and walks down from the choir loft and leaves the services to go home, in broad view of everyone. I doubt there is a pastor alive who has not experienced the protesting "walk out" after Sunday School. However, his story is an excellent example of a conflict that will escalate into conflict or result in persons leaving the church, unless reconciliation occurs. Her actions may seem harmless and insignificant, but her witness is adversely affected by her actions. Particularly troubling is the attitude toward her pastor, her spiritual authority.

Jude, the other half-brother of Jesus, confronts false teachers in the church who were guilty of several indiscretions, one of which was impeding the ministry of the church by their rejection of spiritual authority.[86] Their personal experiences and their own vision for the church overrode the authority of God's revelation. These rebellious people were grumbling faultfinders and arrogant people-flatterers, seeking their own advantage.[87]

Paul reminds the Romans that, "whoever resists authority has opposed the ordinance of God; and

[86] Jude 8.

[87] Jude 16.

they who have opposed will receive condemnation upon themselves."[88] Believers must recognize that if we reject God's authority, then God will reject us. Allow the Lord Jesus Himself to have the final word on spiritual authority, "Truly, truly, I say to you, he who receives whomever I send receives Me; and he who receives Me receives Him who sent Me."[89]

If the church is to move past its passive aggressive behavior, this hindrance to the furtherance of the gospel, then we must put an end to our selfish behavior, reject our cultural programming, and sit down and have a constructive conversation. I think that if believers would lock themselves in a room, talk to each other, pray with each other, demonstrate love toward each other, and allow the Holy Spirit to correct our errant hearts, then we will see a stop to this petty, passive aggressive behavior in the church. Perhaps, this "Lock and Talk" model would produce some real positive change.

The longer you stay in that ministry setting, the more influence you have, the more power and control you have over your church's direction because most of the people in your church came into your church during your ministry. Passive-aggressive behavior is one tactic to challenge your authority and influence. With that said, I have some advice for the long-tenured pastor.

---

[88] Romans 13:2.

[89] John 13:20.

Advice to the Long-Tenured Pastor

A number of recent articles suggest that long-tenured pastors are not the most effective revitalization leaders, which may generally be true, but don't listen to those who say you cannot lead revitalization! Leading an effort like this can be done, but it is certainly a challenge. The problem with long-tenured leaders is that very little of what these leaders do is new and fresh to their churches. Church members have seen it all before, they have heard it all before, and very little that comes from a long-tenured leader is new. Revitalization leaders are attempting to bring something fresh and new to a situation that needs fresh and new. As a pastor of twenty-four years in the same church, I have a few suggestions, which I believe are critical to the success of revitalization ministry.

Freshness Counts

Careful attention to sermon preparation is vital in staying fresh before your congregation. Your church knows all your stories, your illustrations, your sayings, and even your jokes, so you must work hard to develop newness in these areas. Over time, ministers can become a little sloppy, lazy, or unimaginative when writing and delivering their sermons. Do people notice how hard you work at your preaching? I am not talking about people complimenting you for delivering a good Sunday sermon; I am asking you if people see the passionate pursuit of God, the thoroughness of your study, and your effort in communicating the biblical application? What would happen if we, as ministers, would continue to improve in our ministries?

Work On Your Skill Set

Revitalization leaders constantly develop their leadership abilities by improving themselves. Recently, I received some training in the area of coaching, which is a vital part of pastoral development in church revitalization. A coach helps the revitalizer to concentrate on areas that need improvement, develop a strategic plan for revitalization, and stay on the task of implementing that plan. The coaching training I received helped me to develop my listening skills and my ability to ask good questions to those I coach in revitalization. A careful study of the construction of the Old Testament tabernacle reminds us that God uses skillful people in His important work.[90]

The Stalemate Fate

When you know just how far you can push your church, and your church knows how far they can push you, a stalemate occurs, which will test the progress of your church's ministry and will test the love you have for each other. Only with a renewed vision, an acute awareness of your calling, and a desire to be obedient to the Lord, can you work through the stalemate. God has placed the pastor into the life of the church to move the church forward to accomplish

---

[90] C.f. Exodus 36.

its mission, His mission. The pastor's relationship with the Lord supersedes the pastor's relationship with his church. At times, the pastor may need to test the boundaries of his church's love. Remember, God did not call you to be the cruise director of the Love Boat; He called you to be the captain of a battleship with an important mission. He called you to lead your crew into the battle!

The Fear Factor

I know that some of you are thinking that if you push too hard, you could be fired, but remember, pastors serve at the pleasure of the King of Kings; you are employed by Him. God put you where you are to be the shepherd and He can keep you there. Your sheep want to follow a Spirit-led, confident shepherd. When you are following your shepherd, you really don't have to worry about your church following theirs! As a long-tenured pastor, you know your sheep will follow you. Fear keeps us from pursuing worthy goals and our Lord's calling. If you commit enough mistakes, you will experience another problem.

The Cumulative Mistake Factor

One unfortunate result of being a long-tenured pastor is that your mistakes become cumulative; in essence, they all add up. If you serve as the pastor of a church for twenty years, you will make a lot of mistakes! Let me suggest this – get very good at admitting your mistakes and asking for forgiveness. But apologizing for mistakes is not enough, we must learn from our mistakes, rectify them, and if necessary, even make restitution for them. If you do not learn from your mistakes, then over the course of many years, the people that you lead will begin to notice something alarming.

The Repeating Pattern

If you continually make the same mistakes again and again, the people in your church will begin to recognize certain patterns in your ministry and in the life of the church. Certain patterns begin to emerge which become obvious to our church members, who begin to recognize a cause-and-effect pattern in your behavior. They would say, "the last two times we did *x*, we saw *y* happen to our church." They are probably correct in their observations. If you make the same mistakes, you will certainly get a similar series of outcomes. This is where *newness* and *learning from your mistakes* come back into the process of leading the church in revitalization.

How Is Your Fight?

Someone once said, "It's not the size of the dog in the fight, it's the size of the fight in the dog!" Nothing could be more true for church revitalization. Perhaps the biggest reason for the lack of success with long-tenured revitalizers is the amount of commitment and energy required for the project. If church revitalization were a boxing match, it would probably be a fifteen rounder! Church Revitalization requires dogged determination, and those who are patient plodders are ideally suited to the task.

Long-tenured revitalizers may be a vast, untapped resource if they can be properly motivated to get into the fight! These individuals have years of experience in pastoral ministry, which is an incredible asset in revitalization! They also have acquired wisdom, developed relationships, have a network of resources, as well as unmatched insight into the inner workings of their churches. Many of these long-tenured pastors need a rest, a sabbatical, or a retreat to pray about their next 1,000 days (the minimum necessary for a revitalization project). There are certain obstacles to overcome, to be sure, but I believe we should engage these amazing leaders and invite them into the process. Perhaps, if they are refreshed, if they listen to the Lord, and if they are properly encouraged, they may hear God's new calling on their lives – to lead revitalization right where they are.

CHAPTER 9
Revitalization is a Character Issue

While leading ChurchRevitalizer.com I have noticed that of all the necessary components of revitalization leadership, character is the most important. For the past several years, I have worked on church revitalization with pastoral leaders in all sizes of churches and in various stages of their church life-cycles. One important observation I can share is that character, or the lack of it, is one of the prime causes of churches being in their condition. Character is also a prime indicator of whether a church can climb out the hole that it has dug for itself as well.

Think of character, the representation of one's integrity and passion, as the broad base at the bottom of a pyramid. It comes first; without it, nothing else really matters. Character is the foundation that supports everything else in revitalization ministry.

Upon that foundation of character rests personality, which includes disposition (one's usual attitude), professionalism, and approachability. Above that level rests one's education, knowledge, and experience. Finally at the top, representing the smallest component of them all – is one's skills and abilities. I am frequently asked what skills are required, or what do revitalizers need to know, as they lead their churches. More and more, my answer is less about their skills or knowledge, and more about the character that is required to lead such a venture. So, let's talk about character from the biblical perspective, the work ethic perspective, and then the personal diligence perspective (assiduity).

Ezekiel's oracle to the wicked shepherds ought to be considered in our understanding of the character of leaders. God declared His dissatisfaction with the shepherds of Israel. The shepherds were guilty of three grievous crimes that I see duplicated in modern ministry. First, the shepherds were providing for themselves and ignoring their flock.[91] In essence, the sheep were getting what was left over after the shepherds had provided first for themselves. The shepherd exists for the flock; the flocks do not exist for the shepherd! Second, the shepherds neglected the pastoral care of their flocks.[92] They did not care for the sick, treat the sheep with broken bones, or even

---

[91] Ezekiel 34:1-3, 18-19.

[92] Ezekiel 34:4.

pursue the scattered. They had adopted the philosophy that so many pastoral leaders have adopted – it is easier to get new sheep than fix or go after old ones! The third crime was that they did not protect their sheep. The sheep were easy prey because they were scattered. Pastoral leaders rationalize it this way – some sheep fall prey because there are predators. In reality the sheep were prey because the shepherds were too busy feeding themselves to notice those preying on the sheep. Shepherds exist to deal with the predators; sheep should never have this concern.

As you know, a good work ethic is essential to a successful anything! If you do not like to work, then do not go into church revitalization. It is grunt work; non-glamorous, tedious, and wonderful! If you go into revitalization work, forget short work days, frequent golf outings, long vacations, and taking off when you want. Revitalizers need work gloves, not golf gloves. Troubled churches are in need of one thing, and a lot of it – your time. It takes time to process and cultivate the vision that God gives you. It takes time to build the necessary relationships. It takes time to develop the leaders that you will need in the future. It takes time to cast your vision and allow it to take root in the people. It takes time for God to transform your people into usable vessels. It takes time to address the problems, conflicts, and opposition that will present themselves as you begin working on your project. We mistakenly assume that because Nehemiah rebuilt the walls of Jerusalem in only fifty-two days that we can hurry into (and through) the revitalization process. The reality is that the whole work, of which the walls were only a tiny part, lasted thirteen years. Nehemiah heard the news from his brother in 445 BC and the book ends as he institutes the religious reforms in 432 BC. Most of those thirteen years cannot even be accounted for in the pages of scripture. What was Nehemiah doing? Working. In the same manner, we can only account for a few days in Jesus' life. What was the Lord doing the other unaccounted days? He was working.[93]

Another requirement for revitalization character is personal diligence. *Diligence* describes the attention and care required to accomplish something. A synonym for diligence is *assiduity*, which may be an even better way to describe what is required. *Assiduity* is persistent personal attention. Pastoral leaders often lack this quality. We attribute our lack of diligence to medical conditions, such as A.D.H.D., or to personality types. Some things may simply bore us. However, the fact remains that some things have to be done; as tedious as they are, they have to be done. Though well-intentioned, we tend to hop from one great idea to another, just as a frog hops from one lily pad to another. Or we are like the little kid we take fishing that cannot even sit still long enough to keep his line in the water. I was recently helping a pastor in a revitalization project with his church. He asked for some help with the first few steps, so I prescribed four simple activities that would get the project off to a great start. Each of the assigned projects would require less than one hour to complete. We spoke

---

[93] C.f. John 4:34; 17:4.

again two weeks later, and he informed me that he decided that he was only going to do one of the projects. As of last report, he still has not completed that one either. I believe his church is failing in part because he is not even able to do what is expected. Jesus had the same problem with His disciples when He returned and found them sleeping when He declared: *Could you not keep watch one hour?* [94]

Church Revitalization Leader, sit down, slow down, and hunker down. This is going to take a while. Take a deep breath and firm up your personal resolve. Develop this character quality in yourself. Make yourself start revitalization and then make yourself stick to it.

Church Revitalization will reveal your character and build your character as well. Look again at the pyramid example. Of the four categories in the pyramid, the only one that is a good predictor of effective results is Character. Your "gift of gab" will only take you so far. Your charismatic personality will wear thin in your second decade of leading the same group (believe me). Your years of experience, your numerous degrees, and your highly developed skill set mean nothing if there is not passionate, persistent character to go with them.

---

[94] Mark 13:47.

CHAPTER 10
The Fly and the Flypaper: How the Stuck Church Gets Unstuck

While leading RenovateConference.org, I have noticed that in the frenzied era from 1965-1975 we saw the nine mainline denominations within North America decline in many ways! For the first time in American history these major assemblies stopped growing and began to reduce in size. In 1967 Southern Baptists overtook the Methodists, becoming the nation's largest evangelical protestant body. Yet nearly fifty years later even Southern Baptists are faced with continual decline and plateauing of the church's membership and attendance. I am a Southern Baptist and have been one since the day I was saved and invited Jesus Christ into my heart and life. I came to know Christ during the evangelistic efforts of Southern Baptist known as Bold Missions Thrust. Since that time we have been a growing evangelistic denomination. Until recently that is. The President and Executive Director of the SBC, Dr. Frank Page, stated recently that the Southern Baptist Convention is rapidly dying. He further went on to say that our resistance to change could even kill over half of this denomination's churches by 2030, unless something is done to reverse the downward trend.[95] If you take the time to consider his conclusion it is alarming- to say the least - to consider such an evangelical group decline from 48,000+ churches to

---

[95] Baptist Press Posting, May 6, 2008 "Half of SBC Churches Might Die By 2030".

less than 20,000 churches in just over a twenty-two year interlude. The growth from the 1950's has progressively slowed. Church membership is clearly moving to a plateau. Many have predicted that membership would soon began to decline, but the statement, "Southern Baptists are a declining denomination" was not "officially" accurate. Until today![96] From 1999 to 2005, 70,000 protestant churches were evaluated and it was discovered that those churches that declined in growth by more than 10 percent in attendance over that six-year period included 52 percent of the sample. Only 31 percent of the samples were found to be growing over 10 percent in that same six-year time period.[97] The other 17 percent would be those churches that are either stalled or plateaued. Like hapless characters in a B-grade science fiction movie, evangelical churches in America are going through an incredible shrinking act that defies every effort to stop it, says Frank Page. Membership across the country is plateaued or declining. The church, its budget, and its influence in the community are shriveling, sometimes to microscopic size.[98]

---

[96]Ed Stetzer.com Blog, April 20, 2008 posting. Ed is Missiologist in Residence for LifeWay Christian Resources.

[97] David T. Olson, *The American Church in Crisis* (Grand Rapids, MI: Zondervan, 2008), Pgs. 131-132.

[98] Frank Page, *The Incredible Shrinking Church* (Nashville, TN: B & H Publishing Group, 2008), Pg. 7.

Part of the solution rests in moving from attractional models and methodologies to becoming more and more outwardly focused. Many of the stuck churches find themselves ministering more and more only within the walls of the church and the idea of community transformation has become foreign. Since 2000 there has been a decline in every state except Hawaii in Christian church attendance.[99] In churches categorized by size, only new churches with 0-49 attendants and larger churches with 1000 or more attendants is there any display of growth today.[100] Sandwiched in between these two polar opposites are the stuck churches within western Christianity.

"There is a revitalization of Spirituality everywhere, except within the neighborhood house of worship!"
Tom Cheyney@ RenovateConference.org.

The Western Church is in decline and a growing proportion of these churches are stuck on dead center with little or no growth or even decline. Perhaps it is as simple as being stuck on old models, but I think though that is part of it, it is not all of it. While the attractional model appears to be failing some churches, it is vibrant in others. Yet the whole issue

---

[99] For further research go to www.TheAmericanChurch.org and open The American Church Research Project by David T. Olson.

[100] For further research go to www.TheAmericanChurch.org and open The American Church Research Project by David T. Olson.

of becoming stuck is rather large and while I believe there is help within this chapter, further discussion and development needs to continue. For some churches, they are stuck still in the 70's and have no hope of growth in the near future. There are issues that cause a church to become stuck. Sometimes it is the dumb things or the wrong things we do as leaders that kill a church's growth. Other times it is something within the membership in regard to holding on to a church in yester years that can stick a church. I know one church (and many others for that matter) that as the membership is advancing in years and going on to glory, there is a feeling if not an actual commandment to take their church on to glory with them. That is a sad reality for many churches. While there is time for the love of Christ please consider these options and solutions to that type of stuck church.

For the remainder of churches that are not that far gone, this chapter can begin to provide you with some doable solutions and beginning actions or activities that with God's leading and a willing membership, can move off the stuck sandbar of church decline and provide ideas for moving forward and growing once again.

The Beginning of Stuckness

It is easy for a shoot-from-the-hip type leader to lead a new church or even go to another church and pull out his bag of tricks all over again! We have seen within almost any denomination ministers who can pull off a three- to five-year ministry over and over again for their entire ministry career. It is entirely something new for a leader to stay with a ministry and mission that is hard and see it through to the best days of the church's life! Today's true church revitalizer has a call upon his life to see it through and work effortlessly each and every day in a prayerful determination to bring about renewal for the single church God has called them to serve. Instead of people looking back and remembering when the good ole days were here, you can look forward and see the hand of God revitalizing a declining church and moving it off of that dead center or stuck feeling.

The Unrelenting Leader

It is worth noting that it is not the aggressive, shoot-from-the-hip type of leader that makes a strong leader for church revitalization! Rather, the best way to confront momentous troubles within a congregation may be faced and overcome by a single confident unrelenting leader that stays at the task of revitalization and renewal. The best solution either to a predicament or a long-term issue that threatens the well-being of any church is understanding the issues that are causing the struggles and seeking to bring about change in these specific situations.

Examples from life:
- In most community challenges, it is a single leader that emerges to bring order and change.
- Most military conflicts are resolved upon the emergence of an unrelenting key leader!
- Most businesses that flourish and endure are

led by a single individual!

- Most turnaround efforts in the world of commerce are led by a new leader that changes up the status quo and offers hope.
- Most glory days of almost anything are initiated during the tenure of one leader who has vision, foresight, determination, and tenacity!

How did God deal with crisis and stagnation in biblical times? When the children of Israel were languishing in Egypt, God raised up Moses as their leader.

A thought worth taking into consideration: in each and every case God summoned, God empowered, God trained, God deployed, and God encouraged a sole, unrelenting leader!

When the remnant of Israel returned from Babylon and found Jerusalem in ruins, God used the Prophet Nehemiah to focus His children and challenge them with the specific task of rebuilding the walls around the city. When God wanted to spread the Gospel throughout Asia Minor and Europe; how did God respond? God would call an unrelenting single leader in the Apostle Paul to spread the Gospel through the planting of churches.

Churches will prosper and grow in vitality when the right individual leader emerges. God will assist church leaders who are willing to step forward, accept authority, learn, persist, and be responsible! A key leader emerging is the beginning solution to any church revitalization effort. It might not be the person we expect. Many a church revitalization effort is led by a leader other than the shepherd in the pulpit. God often uses the number two staff member or a highly significant lay person to lead the effort of revitalization and renewal. Here is one of the hardest questions to consider as the pastor of a local church that is stuck, in rapid decline, and that needs to begin to grow again. Are you able as a pastor to allow God to use someone else to help you revitalize His church?

What Does "Stuck" Mean in Church Revitalization?

Everyone wants to know if their church is stuck or not. Those who already know they are stuck want to know just how badly they are stuck and what can be done about it. Stuckness usually results in permissiveness of a high degree of polarization to exist for a long time. There are numerous terms that define the need for revitalization from a church trapped in neglect or decay. Here are a few that are often considered:

The Stagnant Church

A stagnant church is one that becomes rather sluggish and is unable to accomplish many of the things it easily accomplished in the past. This immobility causes the church to appear rather stale and lifeless to the few visitors who do happen upon the church. Things appear quite difficult to achieve and even those who are regulars know it but prefer to avoid acknowledgement.

The Sleeping Church

The sleeping church is one that is napping and full of latent activities that keep the church in hibernation. These churches are full of specific events designed to cater to the rapidly declining membership with little focus on those in the community they are called to reach. For the occasional visitor, this type of church appears sluggish, slothful and lazy.

The Idle Church

The idle church is neither declining nor growing. Its stagnancy is gripping to the fear of not knowing what to do. Today, many a church with lay leadership who, in the past knew of ways to strengthen and grow a church, now do not have such participants and those left are stuck in shiftlessness doing little or nothing. Things are stalled in this church and something needs to happen to break it free from its current state.

The Rusting Church

The rusting church is a quandary to me really. There are so many of these in the western culture. The reason they are a quandary is because most of the things that lead to them becoming rust buckets could be easily avoided. Yet, due to a set of polarization issues such as firing of pastors, dismissal of staff, cancelation of programs, and a failure to remain evangelistically active in their community, they have become the beautiful old building in the middle of town that does not try to impact it any longer. Dwindling activities have pushed people from the church instead of pulling them to it. The deterioration of the generations that once participated in this church has made it more of a castle or museum rather than a church set on reaching its community. Mishandling of the ministry has caused decline. Neglect has led to a collapse of the very participants and programs necessary to revitalize the church.

The Dormant Church

The dormant church is still there and appears to be alive but it is not an active church. The membership within this type of church expects the pastor to do everything while they sit back and complain about his efforts towards keeping the doors of the church open. They are incapable of activity and they, for a clearer description, seem inoperative. They appear as if they are in a state of biological rest characterized by cessation of growth. They have not become an extinct church yet but they are also not exploding with new programs and ideas with which to reach out to community. Their church metabolism is held in suspended animation. These churches can become activated once again but it will take a strong gifted church revitalizer who has deep gifts of personal evangelism and relationship building into the community. Think for a minute: Have you ever been part of an organization that emerged from a period of dormancy into new vitality without the dynamic leadership of one or two key individuals? Consider further: Have you ever heard of an organization that was renewed without the dynamic leadership of one or two people who took charge? Here are some non-dormancy indicators you might want to consider. Does the church not have new membership additions equaling at least 10% of its participating membership?[101] Does the church have at least 20% of its active membership exiting through the back door annually? If so you are probably in decline. Have you shut down any ministries such as youth program, nursery, or some adult Bible classes? Sometimes you manufacture the "alive" feeling when it is not there. An example is this: The first year of a new minister in a church has 30 additional people in attendance. Then the next year, attendance drops off significantly. You begin to compare your church with other churches to determine if you are stuck or not. We all must realize that to some measure every church is stuck and to some extent nearly every church is alive!

The Paralyzed Church

The paralyzed church just simply does not feel anything. It neither has a negative emotion for the lost of the community nor a positive one! When one is paralyzed they do not feel anything. Imagine an entire church that feels that way regarding its impact in reaching their community for Christ Jesus. They are helpless and unable to move.

---

[101] Unless you are a Quaker church where this would not be the case.

The Fading Church

The fading church is a waning church full of inactivity. The brightness it once held so dearly is lost. The ministry is dimming and the fresh vision and vigor it once held is gone. It is dying gradually and fading away. They have lost the will to begin the turnaround effort.

The Declining Church

The declining church is a church with a marked decline in weekly church attendance. It is slow at first but eventually it moves the church towards closure. Church participants attend less regularly then they did in the 1940's through 1960's.

The Dying Church

The dying church is one drawing to a close and about to die. Almost every one working in Church Revitalization and Renewal has participated in a conversation of some sort discussing what can kill a church. Think upon some of the things any church can do that will kill it and bring about death. When you emphasize smallness over growth and expansion you can kill the church. In these churches, you may have even heard someone declare how much God loves a tiny church and when growth begins to happen, lament about how much they loved the small personable church.

The All-But-Dead Church

The all-but-dead church is on life support. It is a candidate for the church revitalization restart strategy. This type of church has fallen to below 50 regularly active adult members and is just trying to keep its doors open. Often the people of this church will not want to talk to any one who could help them until it is too late and very little can be done besides giving the facility over to a network of churches or a church plant. They are weary and worn out and just don't have the capacity to live any longer.

To be fair, there are times when an organization is renewed by forces other than an individual leader. If a new business venture moves into one's community and hires five thousand new workers, many of these will be moving into your area and the growth of the churches there will be largely due to the influx of population growth. Sometimes churches renew as the result of a significant staff member.

For instance, the church I belonged to while living in Atlanta has just gone through a period of extreme difficulty and while I am sure the former pastor believed he was the real reason it was renewed, without a doubt the majority of members understood and realize that other forces actually revitalized the church. A few particulars were that the laity loved the church so much it reached out to become more inclusive. That community is in the top three fastest growing counties in the nation, and the membership sacrificed greatly to extend the church and keep it afloat.

What You Have to Change Your Stuck Church!

If change is going to happen in any of these stuck church types you must keep the subject of church revitalization and renewal current. You must begin a long-term crusade that will take around three years. I say it all the time if you are not willing to invest a minimum of one thousand days into revitalization of your church do not begin the journey. You must take small steps and be happy with small victories. Persistence will be a key factor in the revitalization of your church. Try to discover why the church got stuck and what were the things that broke the momentum. As the church revitalizer, you need to be willing to become the change agent while staying focused. Your job as the church revitalizer is to remain calm while everyone else is freaking out. Develop the ability to keep the goal and not become deterred.

Church Revitalization Myths by Any Other Name!

There are always a lot of myths you have to work through when it comes to what will really help you revitalize your church!

The truth of the following statement has always amazed me: If you do what you have always done, you will get what you have always gotten! Yet the guiding principle behind most attempts at revitalization and problem solving in a church seek to follow a predictable set of myths that are exactly that – myths! In fact, merely repeating old blunders, misdirection, or slip-ups will never lead to lasting vitality. Even though you might try harder, the effort will still be the same. Church revitalization myths by any other name are still myths never-the-less.

Change must take place from within and the church as a whole must work at it with everything it has. Less than total effort will lead to little or no success and will wear you and your members out. Recapturing the former luster may not be the end result that is needed so walk carefully and do not place preconceived expectations on what God has planned.

Breaking the Cycle of Discontent and Stagnation

What needs to be broken is the cycle of discontent and stagnation! The tractor pull model, the relight the fire model and the specialist model usually just do not work. Status quo usually wins out over enthusiastic quick strikes that fizzle in the end! Stirring up a congregation without any real long-term effect only wears them out. You must get at the true underlying symptoms and diseases for change to happen.

Let me share with you an interesting story from my home church when I lived in Atlanta. Years ago, we had a vibrant youth ministry supported by a minister which was anything but razzle dazzle! The kids loved him and the youth ministry flourished because of his love for them and their families. A new preacher came in to lead the church and moved the previous youth minister to pastor care and missions. Today, what was a vibrant youth ministry, is dribble at best. Yes they have a cooler, more eloquent minister that their leader likes but the numbers dwindle more and more each year! Not surprising to me but shocking to the younger senior minister is the fact that now almost all of the families that built the church and were faithful for eighteen plus years, have left the church.

Sometimes we substitute the excitement and glitter of a big bang for healing that the majority of congregants needed but never got with the ousting of one minister of youth for another. In fact, the former youth minister is now also their mission's minister and those who are still here from that time usually support whatever he is doing and the new staff are astonished why they don't have a similar following.

Actually, the healing never took place and the members are united around the former minister of youth and still fully supportive of him. The lead minister struggles to develop loyal congregants still and yet the other guy is growing that church.

Bobby Gruenewald, who serves as the innovation pastor at LifeChurch in Edmond, Oklahoma offers four ways to jump start your church's creative thinking when he suggests that you first embrace your current limitations and expect God to show up; set new constraints then challenge people to create their way out of them; empower creative authority; and change the way you view failure.[102]

---

[102] Gruenewald, Bobby. *"Idealing for the World: 4 Ways to*

Much can be learned about the church and its health by careful observation between the key committed membership and the senior pastor. Often a leader in trouble will begin to place huge emphasis on the fringe participants in hope to revitalize his leadership within a church. Remember they are not called fringe participants for nothing. Leaders must learn to stay connected with the runners and not the watchers when things get tough! Far too many pastors who have ostracized the majority of the movers and shakers within an existing church make every attempt to rise up fringe members or even fringe participants in an attempt to reconsolidate one's leadership platform.

The Closed Fortress Effect

A failing marriage is a serious thing for any husband and wife! It is also a serious situation when a church's laity feels separated from its lead minister. When this arises, usually the lead pastor will try to "circle the wagons" to use a visual by drawing, with only a few staff around him and simply become a closed fortress with very few windows. No one can see in and no one can see out! The result is that the additional staff that could help him is not even given the chance to help work out of the situation they find themselves in. Seclusion will foster a growing degree of distrust from the laity and eventually the leader will

Jumpstart Creative Thinking", Outreach Magazine January/February 2008, pgs. 76-78.

come to realize that he has no ability to rally the congregation on any idea, and it is useless to try to do so until the underlying issues are confronted and settled. Leaders who fail to keep open lines of communications open with everyone will eventually be ministering to no one. A great lesson for ministry that John Maxwell taught me years ago as a pastor was, "Do not let what people think about you effect what you think about them!" That has always served me well in these circumstances and helped me to remain open to everyone and run with the runners, even when we did not see everything exactly the same way.

My discovery from asking nearly three thousand lay people, pastors, and church planters the hard questions regarding church revitalization over the last twenty years is that most people answer these questions with great denial to reality. It is as if they are living in a dreamland. God usually wants churches to go on living and thriving. God is on the side of leaders willing to make that happen. A church revitalization minister who has taught me so very much about church renewal and revitalization has been Dr. Mike Simpson, Pastor of First Christian Church in Greensboro, North Carolina reminds us that the qualities of a great church revitalization leader are:

1. Vision for leading the church through the change needed to un-stick a stuck church.
2. Persistence and willingness to remain calm in the midst of turmoil.
3. The ability to anticipate resistance and

sabotage.

4. Playfulness in the stressful times.
5. The ability to stay connected with everyone during the hard times.
6. The ability to be an anxiety shock absorber.
7. Possesses and displays emotional Teflon.
8. The ability to tell the difference between content and process (Content is the stuff people argue about, process is the emotional reality). [103]

Wrapping It Up!

The challenge of a church revitalization leader is not to impart renewal ability into your people, but to extract it, for the capacity is already there. Pastor, if your church is in downward spiral of plateau and decline check some of these indicators out. In western Christianity, there is a new factor that is alarming to say the least if not unscriptural. Some congregations have decided or are deciding right now that it is easier to die rather than live. Far too many churches are attended and led mostly by people who are quite happy for their church to plateau, decline, and die. They recognize that they are personally getting older and will eventually die, and their expectation is that their church will decline with them and also eventually expire. They have no vision for the church being revitalized and no resolve to make

---

[103] Mike Simpson, *The Lazarus Project: How You Can Renew Your Congregation* (Greensboro, North Carolina: 2nd Wind Press, 1999), Pg. 109.

any of the changes that might be necessary for this to happen. Indeed they resist change of any kind. They welcome new members, including younger ones, but only if these people conform to the way things have always been done.

The Problems and Issues of Declining Churches

There is an ever-growing problem with declining attendance and membership in the church today! Once a church begins to become stuck it must work hard at overcoming such a crippling obstacle. There are a whole host of problems and issues when it comes to tackling stuckness within a church that eventually leads to decline:

1. Because Churches can be elderly heavy, or elderly members hold the positions of control, it becomes extremely complicated to make changes. This is especially so as the benefits of doing so are often a long time in coming.

2. Dealing with stuckness means a lot of work, and there are often few people who have both the time and the leaning to take on all the extra work. This means that burnout can happen rapidly, and initiatives fail as the two or three people become dispirited that their efforts seem to be producing less than acceptable results.

3. Often a church's inability to adapt to the changing cultural mix within its ministry area will lead to eventual stuckness. Our world is changing and any church that refuses to change along with it will one

day find itself struggling to overcome the sense of decline, plateau and the feeling of being stuck!

4. It is impossible to keep everyone happy. There is often a huge difference in worshipping styles of the old and the young. Maintaining a 'something for everyone' style can sometimes work, or certainly seem to work initially, but as one or other group tends to be larger, this practice can often slip, or those that were willing to put up with it previously, vote with their feet and go where their needs can be met.

5. If a stuck church finds itself in a socially and economically deprived area, people tend to take much longer to change their mindsets. This means that a church must provide them with something they need, or like. This could include some form of community, friendships, advice, or support systems. If the Church cannot give them something to hold their interest, or address a felt need, they usually will drift.

6. Many stuck churches are unable to fight off the disease feeling of stuckness. They are unable to delay the decay that is fast approaching. The sense of diminished impact and continual deterioration stalls the church and a feeling of being stuck dead center begins to drift in and cause the church to become less of an impact.

7. Most of these stuck churches don't have the luxury of a full-time minister anymore; this removes the figurehead from the church, the central role of authority. Changing the way a whole army of lay volunteers (who do a fantastic job) do things is almost

impossible, so there is often no consistency in a church service from week to week.

8. Financially, most stuck churches are not doing so well. Some have reserves, but live in fear of eating into them as this would then make them financially unsound. Couple this with low attendance and we are talking church closure.

Is there any hope for a stuck church in this condition? Well, nothing is impossible with God, and He could revive such a church with his Holy Spirit. Some things that work usually and have worked in the past are: when a new younger pastor with a strong vision just might be able to get a church going again; when the laity sense one last chance for growth and victory as there is a stirring up of any remaining embers of true spiritual life. Where I serve in central Florida we have one of these churches. It was all but dead and locked into a downward spiral. The change which brought about renewal was when the present leadership realized they were hurting the church and relinquished control to a former pastor who had grown the church significantly. Today this church has grown from twenty-five participants to more than three hundred and fifty participants.

Change is slow and if you are always the first out of the starting gate you will become very frustrated when there will be times where you feel you are beating a dead horse to keep it running! God can restore your church once again! But if you are too hardheaded and hard-hearted to change yourself, then you are probably not able to bring about repair, refocus, renewal, and revitalization. God wants to change His church and He desires to use you and me. Is not that amazing? Our humble dependence coupled with a forward-looking faith might just be all that it will take for God to use you as a renewal participant. You and your church can either be a brief scene from the TV show *Desperate Housewives* or you can watch God lead you forward into greater victory than you have seen in some time. The choice is yours.

Pastor, just as assuredly you will at times in your ministry discover that you have outgrown your people within the congregation; there will be times where they have outgrown you. When this happens, it might be time to re-dream what God wants for this church. Sometimes He will use stuckness to show all of you the way. Watch out for the drift and be cautious with disassociating oneself from the whole membership. Stay engaged while running with the runners. Remember that as a leader any missteps will not only hurt you, but it can also paralyze a congregation so steady goes it at the helm. As you grow in this area of church revitalization you will see yourself taking ownership and responsibility of key transformation projects and making solid renewal decisions. You will also look over your shoulder and discover to your great amazement, that there is still a large contingent of the faithful following joyfully behind you desiring all the time that you lead them out of this predicament and into a greater if not the greatest day for the Lord and His work you call the family of faith right where you live.

A recent study revealed an astonishing fact: There are churches that are 190 to 200 years old that are thriving. They are culturally relevant and lasting relationships are being built each and every day.[104] No church is beyond the power of God to transform it. Remember it is God's timetable and not yours, and it will take some time so be patient. Display a courageous faith daily in the midst of the transformation. Get up and go to work each day allowing the Lord to guide your hands. Though it is daunting and often risky, the uncharted paths move all of us out of those comfortable places into the unsure places where God can stretch us, expand us, grow us and in the end revitalize us once again into a healthy revitalized church. Pray! Pray some more. Now pray even a little more! Lastly, be reassured that the Lord on high will use your church to His glory once again. Remember to give God the praise when He does.

---

[104] Olson, pg.136.

CONCLUSION

The Storms That Come with Revitalization

An Excited Congregation.

One of the most frequently asked questions I get from pastors and churches is, "When can we start church revitalization?" My answer is not the answer they are expecting. I answer. "Not yet!" There are months of spiritual preparation that are needed prior to the official onset of the revitalization project. If this preparation does not happen, the results will be less than impressive. Think of it this way, Nehemiah prayed for four months before he ever approached the King about Jerusalem. He spent another four to five months traveling to Jerusalem from Susa to begin the project. There is every reason for the church to pace itself and to proceed with careful planning and implementation of their revitalization strategy. The church needs to prepare itself for what God intends to do and to prepare itself for the changes that need to take place when God begins to work, and that just takes time.

An Entrenched Leadership.

In their book *Medicine Man Chief*, Renier Greeff and Trevor King described the leadership dynamics of Native American tribes. Their research revealed that although the chief is the identified leader of the tribe, often the real power behind the decision-making lies in the medicine man who can override the chief's decisions and leadership. Often in a revitalization situation, the entrenched leadership of the church prevents the pastor from implementing key changes that are necessary for revitalization. This is a formidable barrier. The entrenched leadership will resist, ridicule, and even enlist others to oppose the revitalization project. If the pastor moves forward with revitalization, then the pastor must either work around these entrenched leaders, discover a way to work with them, or he must drive them away.

An Exasperated Pastor.

The increasing opposition within the church will wear on the pastor. Frequently, the pastor, or the key revitalization leader, will become tired and will run low on energy. If the pastor has served the church for very long, he has certainly encountered his share of challenges and opposition. He has attempted to address the problems of the church, trying every trick he knows. He begins to lose confidence in himself and begins to assume much of the blame for the condition of the church. Without an effective team to help him address the problems and without a mentor or coach to help him implement the new program, the pastor will rarely be successful. A fresh, inspired, and well-motivated pastor is essential in leading a church revitalization project. If revitalization is to be successful, the pastor cannot leave for another church or retire. He must be committed to a long process of three to five years.

An Extraordinary Change.

When the necessary changes begin to happen within the church, the comfort level of the membership will begin to decline – you can be certain of this. The church's organizational structure, practices, and even worship service experience will change. A few people may even abandon the church in this time of crucial change. Though the familiar may be replaced with the effective, the contentment level of the church will definitely change. As church revitalizers, we often hear members say that their church doesn't feel like their church anymore—and that is half the battle! It isn't their church, and it never was! It is the Lord's church. The change is essential if the church is to experience a turnaround. Changing years of practice in the church is risky, but unless the revitalizer is willing to risk, he will never achieve his objectives.

ABOUT THE AUTHORS

Dr. Tom Cheyney
Founder & Directional Leader
Renovate National Church Revitalization
Conference
RenovateConference.org
ChurchRevitalizer.guru
tom@renovateconference.org

Tom is the Founder and Directional Leader of the RENOVATE National Church Revitalization Conference, Executive Editor of *the Church Revitalizer Magazine*, and Co-leader of the RENOVATE Church Revitalization Virtual Coaching Network where he mentors pastors, churches, and denominational leaders in Church Revitalization and Renewal all across North America. He serves as the National Host of the weekly *Church Revitalization and Renewal Podcast*. Dr. Cheyney has written over 4,000 print, audio resources, guides, or books for church revitalizers, pastors, church planters, and lay leaders. His most recent books include *Thirty-Eight Church Revitalization Models for the Twenty First Century* and *Preaching Towards Church Revitalization and Renewal*. Cheyney has written along with his friend Rodney Harrison *Spin-Off Churches* (B&H Publishers). Tom is a nationally recognized conference speaker and a frequent writer on church revitalization, church planting, new church health, and leadership development. Others have label Tom as the *Father of the Church Revitalization Movement* as his influence has stretched across multiple denominations and countries.

Dr. Terry Rials
Pastor and Church Revitalizer
ChurchRevitalizer.com

Terry Rials has been in Christian Ministry for twenty-seven years, the last twenty-four as the Senior Pastor of the Crestview Baptist Church of Oklahoma City. He is a graduate of Oklahoma Baptist University (B.A., Applied Ministries), Southwestern Baptist Theological Seminary (M.Div.BL), and earned his doctorate (D.Min.) from Midwestern Baptist Theological in Church Revitalization. His dissertation project involved training pastors in the principles of revival and revitalization by equipping them to begin a revitalization project in their churches. Rials has studied abroad in Israel, Egypt, and at Oxford University in England. He has taught New Testament courses and Biblical Hermeneutics for Oklahoma Baptist University at its Oklahoma City campus. He is also the Church Revitalization professor for the Master of Arts in Theological Studies program at Midwestern Baptist Theological Seminary and contributes in Doctoral Seminars on campus. Terry has served as a breakout innovator at the Renovate National Church Revitalization Conference, and is a feature writer to *The Church Revitalizer* Magazine.

Dr. Rials serves as the Church Revitalization Team Leader for Capital Baptist Association in Oklahoma City and is active in leading church revitalization efforts in Oklahoma and nationally. He is a frequent conference speaker and teacher.